OUTSWIMMING
THE SHARKS

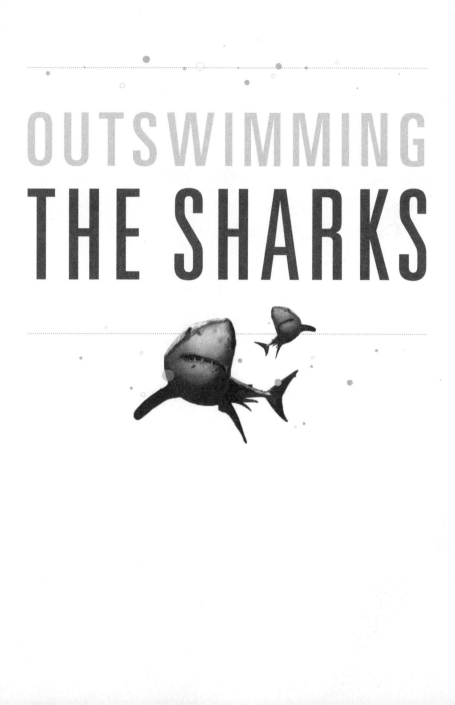

OUTSWIMMING
THE SHARKS

OVERCOMING ADVERSITIES, NAYSAYERS, *and*
OTHER OBSTACLES *to* LEAD *a* MEANINGFUL LIFE

J. H. HYUN

EMERALD
BOOK CO.

Published by Emerald Book Company
Austin, TX
www.emeraldbookcompany.com

Copyright ©2011 Joong H. Hyun

Distributed by Emerald Book Company

For ordering information or special discounts for bulk purchases, please contact
Emerald Book Company at PO Box 91869, Austin, TX 78709, 512.891.6100.

Design and composition by Greenleaf Book Group LLC and Alex Head
Cover design by Greenleaf Book Group LLC

Publisher's Cataloging-In-Publication Data
(Prepared by The Donohue Group, Inc.)
Hyun, J. H. (Joong H.), 1969-
    Outswimming the sharks : overcoming adversities, naysayers, and other
obstacles to lead a meaningful life / J.H. Hyun. — 1st ed.
    p. ; cm.
  ISBN: 978-1-934572-81-8
1. Self-actualization (Psychology) 2. Conduct of life. I. Title.
BF637.S4 H97 2011
158.1   2011922766

Part of the Tree Neutral® program, which offsets the number of trees
consumed in the production and printing of this book by taking proactive steps, such as planting trees in direct proportion to the number of trees used: www.treeneutral.com

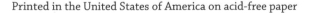

Printed in the United States of America on acid-free paper

11 12 13 14 15 16 10 9 8 7 6 5 4 3 2 1

First Edition

TreeNeutral®

For my beautiful and most precious wife, YoonJeong.

No temptation has overtaken you except what is common to mankind. And God is faithful; he will not let you be tempted beyond what you can bear. But when you are tempted, He will also provide a way out so that you can endure it.

—I Corinthians 10:13

CONTENTS

PREFACE

In the summer of 2006, I was promoted to a vice president position for a multibillion-dollar, U.S.-based, global medical device company. It was a week before my thirty-seventh birthday, and I believe I was the youngest person ever to become a senior executive VP within the organization.

Once the official corporate-wide announcement was made, I received dozens of congratulatory e-mails and phone calls. I must admit that I, too, was pretty proud of myself. The good-wish e-mails, phone calls, and handshakes continued for several weeks, but unfortunately, my self-pride didn't last too long.

On my way home late that same night, I felt a sudden surge of emptiness. The fact that there was no one at home to greet me or congratulate me was difficult to accept. The fact that I had no family of my own or any other loved ones immediately available to share the good news with made me question whether I had been climbing the right ladder. In less than twelve hours, what had been the proudest achievement in my professional career had quickly turned into one of the loneliest moments in my life.

I had overcome many naysayers at work, less than ideal family circumstances, prolonged financial struggles, and several other "sharks" in reaching what many would consider worldly success. In my relentless journey to reach the peak of my chosen profession, however, I had forgotten what is truly important in life. I had been, for the most part, meandering through the maze of my own life without a clear focus and ultimate destination in mind. I had allowed other people and events to dictate my direction. I desperately needed to reevaluate and rebalance my priorities.

For the most part, I consider myself extremely fortunate and blessed in many ways. As a naïve child growing up in Seoul, I never imagined I would have the opportunities I have had—the places I have visited, education I have received, people I have met and worked with, positions I have held, and high-level business decisions I have played a part in, to name a few. I know many people who are far more intelligent and competent than I am who have not had these opportunities. For this, I remain truly grateful.

However, like everyone else, I have confronted, and continue to confront, my fair share of sharks. My past sharks include the untimely death of my father, severe and prolonged financial struggles, the shameful and sudden loss of a home, an emotionally draining breakup, unexpected derailment from a promising career, several horrible bosses (whom I believe are closely related to Satan), backstabbing coworkers, borderline insane clients, and loss of self-confidence, self-esteem, and self-worth. Over the years

I have learned to tolerate and even appreciate the presence of these sharks. I no longer expect or wish for a shark-free life. All great achievements in history came about in the midst of and as a reaction to atrocious shark attacks. To reach your full potential, you need formidable sharks to tame and conquer in your life. This is one of the most important and valuable life lessons I have learned. Even if a shark-free life were possible, it wouldn't be worth living.

There will always be sharks in your life to throw you off course and make reaching your full life potential a bit more challenging. I hope this book will help you set the right goals, stay focused on achieving them, and evaluate your progress to ensure that you remain on the right path. You can and must do this regardless of and in the midst of the sharks in your life. This is what it takes to live a meaningful life.

Most lessons discussed in this book are from actual experiences I had, and others are from stories I read or heard that made a profound, lasting impact in my life. Some are humorous, some are a bit unusual, and others were pretty painful and unpleasant to go through—but each situation provided a valuable lesson I wish to share with you. In many instances, the lessons were not clear to me until several years later. Nevertheless, there were definite, valuable lessons gained from all these situations, which helped me to develop and grow as a person. I also have many regrets and have made plenty of mistakes worth sharing to prevent you from repeating them.

In addition to my own experiences, I will draw on others' successes and failures. I have closely observed dozens of successful people. I can't think of a single successful person who didn't have to face, stand tall against, and overcome his or her own set of naysayers, personal tragedies, major setbacks, and many other shark species. These people used their sharks as opportunities to grow personally and to better the lives of others. My decision to write this book provided an opportunity for me to reflect on and evaluate their character, behavior, leadership styles, and habits. On the flip side, I have seen others who never fully achieved levels deserving of their effort, competency, and potential. Summarizing these lessons into an easily digestible format has been an exceptional experience. I hope you will find them useful in reaching your full potential and enriching your life, both professionally and personally.

I am a firm believer that your chosen career path and, more important, your life, need to be planned. Your life also needs to be regularly evaluated and reflected upon, regardless of whether you are a corporate employee, a contractor, a lawyer, a teacher, an athlete, a musician, whatever. After all, life is your most precious gift from our Maker. What you make of this gift is entirely up to you. I hope you will find what I have to share to be inspiring, thought provoking, and helpful in evaluating, prioritizing, and energizing your life.

My main intent for writing this book is to help you succeed in your chosen professional field as well as in your personal life. Swimming with the sharks in pursuit of your life goals can and should be both an exciting and extremely rewarding experience. And there's nothing like outswimming your own set of sharks. You are much stronger and more capable than you give yourself credit for. Sharks in your life are there to be conquered by you. You can and will outswim every shark in your life if you stay focused and work hard toward reaching your goals. Yes, it can be done, and it needs to be done properly.

I have had numerous mentors who guided and supported me along the way. They are my former professors, pastors, bosses, coworkers, family members, and loyal friends. Whether they realize it or not, they helped me put things into perspective, prioritize my life, and extract the valuable lessons from what seemed, at times, to be merely horrible experiences. Although chances are slim that you and I will ever meet in person, I hope to pass along at least some of the wisdom that's been bestowed upon me through these wonderful individuals.

Enjoy the read, and enjoy your time swimming with and outswimming your sharks as you immerse yourself in the pursuit of your ultimate life goals and dreams.

With many thanks,
—J. H. Hyun

INTRODUCTION

Simply put, sharks in this book represent any opposition that we must endure and overcome to achieve our own success and live the life we are capable of living.

Just as there are over four hundred shark species in the ocean, there are just as many potential sharks in our lives. Some examples of sharks in our lives include heartbreaking tragedies, unexpected distractions, less than ideal circumstances, unfortunate mishaps, overwhelming adversities, major setbacks, and what appear to be insurmountable obstacles. Sharks also represent and symbolize the people who prevent us from living our dreams. They are the difficult people you face and deal with on a regular basis who tend to derail you from setting and achieving your life goals. Sharks are your naysayers who demotivate you and cause you to doubt yourself. These are the people who choose to focus on the potential problems rather than the opportunities ahead. Based on what they say and do, they seem fixated on making sure you do not reach your full potential. They may be your boss or coworker, competitor, parent, relative, or so-called friends. In order for us to reach our goals, it is crucial that we overcome the incessant negative messages from these human sharks. Everyone, without exception, has his or her own set of sharks to deal with.

Unfortunately, one of your sharks may also be one of your dearest loved ones giving you well-intended advice. More often than not, such individuals genuinely care for you and are afraid for you. They don't want you to fail, so they advise you to choose the most conservative, safest routes in life. With deep and sincere concern, they warn you against pursuing a particular sport you truly enjoy and excel in because of potential injuries. They advise you against pursuing a career in music or acting because of the slim chances of you ever making it big. They gently and regretfully remind you that your family doesn't have sufficient financial means for you to study law, medicine, or any other desired degree at a top university. Regardless of their intention, these loving people can limit your personal growth and prevent you from dreaming big and living your life to the fullest. As much as they love you, deep down perhaps they are just afraid and jealous of you actually reaching your dreams. It is essential that you recognize these instances when well-meaning people are steering you the wrong way. If you can set a clear goal and are willing to work for it, you can overcome and achieve just about anything in your life.

This book is about living a meaningful and successful life. I have a rather simple view and definition of success. It is setting the right, worthwhile goals and achieving them in an honorable manner.

We all have our own set of sharks in our lives. Life has a habit of throwing these sharks at us. You may be going through a shark attack at this very moment. This book is about maintaining your focus and composure in the midst of your sharks. There is no need to swim away from them. There are reasons for the sharks in our lives. We must swim with and outswim them to attain our goals and live a truly successful life. Facing these sharks can sometimes be frustrating and emotionally draining. But be assured, you can outswim them all. You can achieve your dreams and goals and succeed in life in the midst of, in spite of, and because of these sharks.

You should be grateful for the sharks in your life. There are valuable lessons to be learned from them. Don't let them get the better of you by tainting your attitude or outlook on life. You are bigger than any shark God has allowed in your life. This is a fact I have come to realize after meeting, getting to know, and working closely with many successful people over the past two decades. You need to believe this for yourself. Don't use the sharks in your life as a convenient excuse for your failure. Instead, use them as a necessary stepping-stone to better yourself and to move ahead, to achieve your life goals. You can do this without having to succumb to their ways, without sinking to their level, and without compromising your integrity, values, and beliefs.

Learn to replace your fear of potential failure with the expectation of deserved success. We are often way more capable than we credit ourselves for being. Reaching success and living a meaningful life, in the midst of our sharks, will take focus, passion, and sweat. Let us now begin our journey.

PART I

SUITING UP

CHAPTER 1

HOW DO YOU WANT
TO BE REMEMBERED?

Always go to other people's funerals. Otherwise, they won't come to yours.
—*Yogi Berra, American baseball legend*

As I type these words, we have recently gone through one of the hardest economic downturns in decades. It appears, at least at this point, that the worst is finally over and we are on our way to recovery. The past two years have been deservedly labeled a "financial tsunami." We are all holding our breath that it is truly over. Globally, housing prices have been plunging for the past two years with no clear end in sight. More than $17 trillion has been wiped out in stock markets globally. In the United States alone, millions of jobs were eliminated between 2009 and 2010. The unemployment rate in the United States crossed the 10 percent mark for the first time in decades, more than double the normal rate, which hovers in the low to mid 4 percent range. The experts believe this dismal unemployment figure will remain for at least another twelve to eighteen months. Other more pessimistic views are claiming that an 8 to 9 percent unemployment rate will be the new norm.

Unfortunately, this is not an issue unique to the United States. For now, the global economic landscape remains uncertain at best. Unemployment is an issue facing just about all nations today, and most experts do not expect the situation to improve anytime soon. The economic situations in several European countries, including Spain, Greece, and Ireland, are now at the worst point in recent history. The phrase "jobless recovery" appears to be ubiquitous these days. Now may be a good time to remind ourselves that we are more than the title on the business card we carry (or used to carry). Wanting to succeed and being ambitious are good things, and I encourage both. But you should first define what success means to you and then set goals that are right for you.

What Do You Want on Your Tombstone?

Do you plan to have your list of business titles engraved on your tombstone? I doubt anyone would. After your time in this world comes to an end—and it happens to everyone—how do you want to be remembered? Most people want the epitaph on their tombstone to read something along the lines of "a loving father, husband, brother, loyal friend." I have yet to run across anyone who insists on listing his or her educational background, test scores, awards received, trophies won, cars driven, size of home, annual income, bank account balance at the time of death, projects accomplished (even if they were done on schedule and under budget), or any of the things we stress over so much.

But how do *you* want to be remembered? Think about this for a few minutes and then jot your ideas down on a piece of paper. Order your thoughts so that how you most want to be remembered by the most important people in your life is at the top of your list. Imagine yourself attending your own funeral. You see your own body lying in a casket. There are many people in the room paying their last respects. Only you can see and hear them. What would you want them to say about you? Who would miss you the most? What would they say you treasured the most while you were alive? Keep this list with you, along with three others recommended at the end of this chapter, for the next several months. Whenever you are in doubt as to what direction and actions to take, use this list as a guideline in making the right decisions.

An ex-girlfriend of mine once told me, "If you love me, you should spend more of your time and money on me." Although she said this half jokingly when she was a bit displeased with my work schedule, some of her true feelings were definitely behind the statement.

People spend their time and money on what's important to them. Are you living consistently with how you want to be remembered? Are you spending enough time and money on what's really important to you? Do your actions today align with your ultimate life goals? What do you want on your tombstone?

No Shortcuts

You should not expect to get ahead without working harder than your peers and making sacrifices. Just as a professional athlete or a top musician spends endless hours practicing, to excel in what you do and to get ahead, you must be willing to make a similar commitment.

Regardless of what you decide to commit to, you will need to be prepared to make sacrifices. If you want to move ahead in your career, you will need to put in a few extra work hours during the week and on the weekends. You will need to sacrifice other things you enjoy. If you are a parent, this will mean occasionally missing your child's soccer games or piano recitals.

If you have more of a "work to live" approach to life, and would rather spend more time with your family or pursuing nonprofessional interests than climbing the corporate ladder, then a routine forty hours—or even fewer—may be your best option. There are also sacrifices that come with this decision, as you will most likely have less financial means. The important things to remember are to define your life priorities and to keep a proper balance.

A longtime colleague of mine, whom I have come to admire and respect over the years, once confided in me in tears that his biggest regret in life was not being there when his father passed away. He had made a conscious decision to go on an extremely important overseas business trip while his father was ill and fighting for his life. It was a chance he knowingly took and one he will regret for the rest of his life.

When he shared this story with me, it had been more than a decade since his father's death. My friend is now approaching sixty and nearing the twilight years of his very successful business career. He cried in private as he told me how he had made the wrong choice. He no longer remembered what the meeting was about. He referred to his decade-old decision as one of the biggest regrets of his life.

You should have a clear idea of what you want in life and make your decisions based on how best to achieve your goals. Be ambitious and make the necessary sacrifices—but remember to check against your ultimate life goals. There are things you will never get a chance to redo. You cannot delegate another person to attend a ten-year anniversary dinner, nor do you get to reschedule your loved one's funeral. Learn from someone else's mistakes. Make sure to prioritize what's most important to you and live accordingly each and every day. Be absolutely sure of your final desired destination, and make sure you are not going in the wrong direction.

Recommended Actions

Have you identified what's most important to you? Are you living consistently with how you want to be remembered? Are you spending time and money consistently? The following recommended actions should help you answer these questions.

1. List the names of people who mean the most to you. Make a habit of reviewing and, if necessary, updating this list once every few months as a reminder of the most important people in your life. Stop worrying so much about what others, who are not on this list, think or say about you.

2. Make a list of how you want to be remembered, especially by the people on list 1. Be specific. Imagine yourself attending your own funeral—who do you want to see there? What do you want your loved ones to say about you? If you have a hard time picturing the people on list 1 crying their hearts out at your funeral, you may need serious life adjustments before it's too late.

3. We are all equally given 168 hours per week. Most people spend between 50 and 55 hours sleeping, leaving only about 115 hours available to spend toward whatever we choose. Time is one of the most precious gifts we have been blessed with. Each hour that passes will never come back. Make a list of how you spent this irreplaceable gift last week. Who did you spend the time with? What activities were you involved in? Make a separate list for another week or two, if you believe how you spent your time last week is not a good indication of a typical week.

4. Make a similar list detailing how you spent your money. Include all expenditures, regardless of how you paid. Include even those you believe are one-time, special expenses. If you feel justified, make a separate list for another week or two.

5. Do lists 3 and 4 support lists 1 and 2? If the two sets of lists are out of sync, make another list of how you will spend your time and money next week and going forward.

Repeat the preceding five actions at least once every few weeks for the next three to six months. Are people on list 1 noticing the positive difference? Ask for their feedback.

CHAPTER 2
DREAM BIG

Security is mostly a superstition. It does not exist in nature.
Life is either a daring adventure or nothing.
—Helen Keller, author, political activist, and lecturer who
prevailed over her blindness and deafness

There is a story in the Bible in the book of Matthew, chapter 25, about a man giving each of his three servants money prior to going on a journey. He gives them different amounts, "each according to his ability" (verse 14). Two of the servants put the money to work and earn more money. The last servant chooses to dig a hole in the ground and hide the money (for security purposes, I presume). When the master returns, he is pleased with the first two servants and declares, "Well done, good and faithful servant! You have been faithful with a few things. I will put you in charge of many things. Come and share your master's happiness" (verse 23). The last servant then approaches the man and says: "[I] knew that you are a hard man, harvesting where you have not sown and gathering where you have not scattered seed. So I was afraid and went out and hid your talent [money] in the ground. See, here is what belongs to you" (verses 24 and 25). The man is clearly not happy with the servant who chooses security over opportunity. He responds by exclaiming, "You wicked, lazy servant!" and then demands, "Throw that worthless servant outside, into the darkness, where there will be weeping and gnashing of teeth" (verses 26 and 30). Those are pretty harsh words, especially to someone who securely kept and dutifully returned what had been entrusted to him.

Clearly, we are to use the "talents" we have been given not necessarily to enrich only our own lives but those of others as well. Choosing to do nothing and "playing it safe" are not what our God had in mind when He created us.

When I was a kid reading this parable for the first time, I wondered whether the man would have reacted to the first two servants in the same loving way if they had lost his money. Had this been the situation, I wondered whether the man would have rewarded the third servant for not losing (or gaining) by choosing to do nothing. I don't think this would have been the case. I believe the man was awarding the honest work and the effort, not necessarily the results.

Regardless of what your life goals are, you need to recognize and seize the opportunities to get there. Standing still is easy and comfortable, but it won't get you closer to success. Security sure feels good, but opportunities are worth far more than security or guarantees. Resist the temptation to remain idle. Refuse to become a prisoner of familiarity and comfort.

Fortune favors the brave.
—Virgil, ancient Roman poet

As mentioned earlier, often people who love you are the ones who hinder you from pursuing and achieving your dreams. For the most part, I believe these people do this for the right loving and caring reasons—but there will be a few crucial moments in your life when you should break away and seize the opportunity.

Choose to Believe in Yourself

Many years ago when I first started working in Asia, I got to know a young man whom I could best describe as "PHD"—poor, hungry, and determined. He was a great person, full of energy, positive, highly intelligent, and hard working. He came from a small farming town and was the first and only one to graduate from college out of all his extended family members. I believe he had four or five siblings, over a dozen uncles and aunts, and more than twenty cousins. I had met several of them on occasion. While I sensed at least some level of jealousy from a couple of his siblings, his parents were extremely proud of him and couldn't stop talking to me about their prized son. Unfortunately, these loving family members held him back from pursuing and achieving his dreams. When I first met him, he was struggling with this very issue. He had a very loving family who constantly reminded him that what he had already accomplished was good enough and that it was time to settle for a safe job, get married, and have kids. He was barely twenty-four years old at the time. When I asked what he wanted out of his life, he told me of his desire to see the world, his passion for learning, and his ambitions of earning higher degrees. His eyes lit up as he spoke of his dreams. Clearly this was the path for him. I encouraged him to apply to at least a few of his dream schools.

Less than two years later, I was surprised and disappointed to find out that he had turned down a scholarship for a reputable graduate program and also turned down an offer to work overseas for a couple of years. His loving family did not think returning to school was a good financial choice, especially as he entered his prime marrying age. They were also concerned about the risks and uncertainty associated with working overseas and what would happen after the two-year assignment ended. He had chosen to listen to the right people giving the wrong advice.

I lost touch with him many years ago, but the last I remember, he was bitter about the choices that were "forced" upon him. He was stuck in a boring and unchallenging position at work, and he felt too old to return to university, especially with a wife and two little kids to support. He had long ago lost his dreams; in his own words, he was now "living to support his kids." Although this sounds altruistic, I wonder if his life would have been far more fulfilling if he had chosen to believe in himself a decade earlier.

> *Every affluent father wishes he knew how to give his sons the hardships that made him rich.*
> —Robert Frost, American poet

Listen to your inner voice. You should take advice from others, especially those who love you, but you need to make the decision yourself. Seize the opportunity. Opportunities are worth far more than guarantees. You won't succeed by hiding your "talents" in the ground.

Avoid the "I Can't" Shark

Often, your life's greatest foe is yourself. There is no more formidable opponent. As Harry Truman, thirty-third president of the United States, once stated, "In reading the lives of great men, I found that the first victory they won was over themselves. Self-discipline with all of them came first."

Success starts when you begin to pursue it. You don't need

to know all of the answers in advance to have dreams and to reach them.

Don't shy away when faced with difficult problems. You will encounter many shark attacks in your life. Don't let them distract you from pursuing your dreams. Break your problems into smaller parts, and handle one manageable piece at a time. Take action. Take control and accountability of your own life. Divide your big dreams into small steps and take that first step right away.

Don't be pushed by your problems.
Be led by your dreams.
—Anonymous

Life will give you what you ask for. Have a dream for yourself and work hard. Don't turn yourself into the biggest shark of your own life.

Dream Big

You determine how big or small of an accomplishment you get to achieve in your own life. See in yourself the great potential rather than imposing self-inflicted limitations, and life will give you what you ask for. You are far more capable than you give yourself credit for.

I once read a magazine article in which the writer claimed he had interviewed hundreds of 2008 Olympic medalists from dozens of countries. I have forgotten much of the article, except for one common thread the writer had found in all these winners, without a single exception. All of the world-class athletes had dreamed of competing in the Olympics, and they had all believed they could and would win against the best of the best. The common dream and the unwavering belief, the author concluded, did not guarantee victory, but both were necessary in obtaining it.

> *The only thing that will stop you from fulfilling your dreams is you.*
> *—Tom Bradley, former-slave's grandson who became five-term mayor of Los Angeles*

There are no "accidental" Olympic medalists in life. In the same manner, you won't one day simply run into your own success without having a dream and working relentlessly toward achieving it.

There are reasons for our being in this world. Our Maker has given each of us a set of talents. Fully utilize your talents to enrich the lives of your loved ones. As you reflect on your life to date, have you dreamed big enough in your life? Do you have, and are you pursuing, the right dreams? Are you putting in the required effort to achieve those dreams? Or, heaven forbid, have you hidden your God-given talents in the ground?

I see and meet so many people afraid to pursue their most important dreams. Many feel that they don't deserve them.

Others degrade themselves by concluding they are not good enough to achieve their dreams.

Not reaching your dreams is not the unfortunate thing, but rather, not having a dream to reach for. What are your dreams? Have you allowed your sharks to nibble them away?

Make and Pursue Your Own Dreams

Cornelius Vanderbilt (1794–1877) was the most powerful and successful American businessman of his time. He made his fortune in steamship lines and railroads. He helped build the nation's transportation system. Vanderbilt wasn't well known for philanthropy until late in his life, when he donated a million dollars—an enormous sum back then—to Central University in Nashville, Tennessee. Obviously, this university is now known as Vanderbilt University. At his death more than a hundred years ago, Vanderbilt left an estate valued at $105 million. Even at a modest inflation rate, this equates to well over $1 billion in today's value.

Every great dream begins with a dreamer. Always remember, you have within you the strength, the patience, and the passion to reach for the stars to change the world.
—*Harriet Tubman, American escaped slave, Civil War soldier, abolitionist*

Here's a somewhat surprising ending to this story. According to Arthur T. Vanderbilt II, author of *Fortune's Children: The Fall of the House of Vanderbilt*, when more than one hundred of Cornelius Vanderbilt's descendents gathered at a reunion in 1973, there was not a single millionaire left among them. The money had all been spent. The financial wealth had been transferred without responsibility or accountability. William K. Vanderbilt, grandson of Cornelius, said, "It has left me with nothing to hope for, with nothing definite to seek or strive for." Inherited wealth can be a real handicap to happiness.

What we gain easily can and often will just as easily slip away. This is true with financial wealth as well as just about anything else in life. In the words of Abraham Lincoln, "The worst thing you can do for those you love is the things they could do for themselves." Lack of a head start is not a good reason for not trying or for giving up. Inherited wealth can often result in lack of zeal and determination. Having two world-class athletes as your parents won't compensate for laziness. Set big dreams and pursue them relentlessly regardless of your starting point.

You only live once. It is in your best interest to live to the fullest. This does not mean you should live recklessly. It does not mean you should make foolish choices and gamble with your life. It does mean, however, that you should take advantage of opportunities that come your way. Opportunities are worth far more than guarantees in life.

Each of us should first demolish any and all self-perceived, self-created limitations. Take prudent risks as opportunities arise. Standing still is always a comfortable option and often a common choice. Choose to be one of the few. Take the less traveled road. We are often much more capable than we credit ourselves. We won't know our limits until we push ourselves to them. Dream big.

CHAPTER 3
SET CLEAR AND SPECIFIC DESTINATIONS

The first step toward getting somewhere is to decide
that you are not going to stay where you are.
—J. Pierpont Morgan, banker who dominated corporate finance
and industrial consolidation during his time

The beltway traffic around Washington DC is notorious for its congestion. The traffic can be especially unbearable during the morning and again, without fail, in the evening rush hours. I lived in the northern Virginia area for many years, and on countless occasions I was part of the twice-a-day bumper-to-bumper march. It's a frustrating experience—one I am sure most people living in urban areas can relate to.

Despite the seemingly infinite number of cars and trucks, most drivers, if not all, have definite destinations. During morning traffic, most people are headed to their place of work. Others are on their way to school, to the airport, to meet a friend, to begin a long-awaited family vacation—there are countless possibilities. It's unlikely someone would choose to be part of the daily urban ritual without a specific destination. People select the best routes and roads, change lanes, and make turns based on their ultimate destinations. Some may get lost on the way, but they would not realize they were lost unless they had a clear destination in mind. And only by knowing that you are lost can you promptly correct your course.

Where Are You Now?

Where are you in your life journey? Do you have a definite and ultimate destination for your life? Are you driving aimlessly? Have you stopped questioning where all the meandering will ultimately take you? Are you simply going with the flow? How do you decide whether to continue on the same road or to turn right or left? How do you make important life decisions?

Set clear and specific destinations for your life. These destinations should be your ultimate goals. Consider them your life compass and let them dictate your actions, the proper path you take, and the turns you make in your life journey. In the midst of all your troubles, naysayers, and any other shark species in your life, do not let go of your compass or forget what direction it is pointing.

When setting your goals, start with how you want to be remembered. Set difficult and worthwhile goals—ones that will form you into a better and stronger person, enrich the lives of your loved ones, and inspire others. When I am at a major life crossroad, I refer to my goals and make decisions accordingly. I recently made a decision to leave an organization after five wonderful years. It was a rather difficult and emotional decision, arrived at only after much thought, self-debate, and several months of reflection. I believe I made the right decision—maybe not financially, but in terms of what's truly important in my life and how I want to be remembered when my time is up in this world.

We succeed only as we identify in life, or in war, or in anything else, a single overriding objective, and make all other considerations bend to that one objective.
—Dwight D. Eisenhower, thirty-fourth president of the United States

You see, writing a book was one of my life goals. Following my dream required me to save for several years and to leave the safety of having a steady job for a year.

Even after you have clearly defined your goals, actually achieving them is difficult. But it is possible—especially for anyone with the persistence to stay on track.

After a couple of decades, it still takes conscience effort and a lot of self-discipline for me to devote time to my wife, self-development, writing, visiting family and friends, prayer, and all the other things that are important to me. Spending my time this way is consistent with what's important to me and how I ultimately want to be remembered. Following these goals is demanding and requires me to identify and compromise less important things in my life. That means cutting back on watching sports and surfing the net, especially on the weekends. Without higher priority, worthwhile goals, I would be in my comfortable clothes on my couch glued to the TV every weekend.

In finalizing your life goals—that is, setting your life compass—make sure you consider the following questions:

1. Is the goal consistent with how you want to be remembered?

2. What will it take to achieve the goal? Are you willing to make the required payment in time and sweat? What sacrifices are you willing to make?

3. What obstacles must you overcome? Are you willing and able to ignore the naysayers? What other sharks must you outswim to reach success?

4. Once achieved, will the goal have a long-lasting positive impact on you and others? How will it enrich the life of those you love?

Yes, actually achieving your goals is easier said than done, but it is absolutely doable. Start today and don't stop. Right now you are the youngest you will ever be for the rest of your life. Today is the best day to properly reset your compass and to begin your journey anew.

Is Your Compass Properly Tuned?

I had a stubborn colleague who married relatively early and had two kids before the age of thirty. After his marriage and especially after the arrival of his kids, he wanted so much to provide financially for his family. He had grown up extremely poor and did not want to put his own wife and kids through what he and his family had gone through. His goal was to be financially rich, which in itself was an admirable one.

With increasing his net worth as the overarching (and perhaps only) goal, he jumped from one job to another no fewer than ten times—each time for a higher salary. In fact, he stayed with the consulting company where I first met him for just over a year before moving on to a competing consulting company at a higher level, which paid him almost 15 percent more. Every time he moved on, the new job meant more responsibilities and longer hours, and he regularly worked into nights and weekends. After more than two decades of this "proactive career management," as he used to call it, he is now in his late forties and holds a nice title at a midsize manufacturing firm. He is by no means super-rich, but through hard work and prudent spending, he now has a sizeable savings. Even if he stopped working today, he and his wife could retire fairly comfortably. He also has sufficient financial means to send his kids to top private universities, which is exactly where they both are today. He feels, as he should, proud of what he has done. But as you can guess, this is not the end of the story.

Unfortunately, he will be the first to tell you that if he were to live his life again, he would not make the same decisions. Yes, he has achieved the financial goals he set out to achieve. But getting there required him to make compromises and decisions he would later regret. He feels disconnected from his wife and especially his kids. I ran into him at an airport lounge in Tokyo a couple of years ago. It had been only eight or nine years since we first met, but he had aged greatly during those years, almost beyond recognition. He wondered whether the sacrifices had been worth it. While we worked together many years back, I had seen pictures of his kids when they were just toddlers. Sitting together in the lounge, as he showed me the latest photos of his family on his laptop, he commented that one day he turned around and his kids had grown up. His kids had needed and longed so much for his time and attention while he was busy chasing what he once thought was the right goal. He still loved them, but they had grown apart. He had become, at least in his mind, a mere source of financial support for his wife and kids.

Being the great analyst he is, my former colleague had calculated how much he had gained by constantly job hopping for better pay and more responsibilities; he was a full three years ahead financially of where he would have been had he stayed with his fourth company (where we met). Was it worth it? Were the three years of monetary gains worth the loss of more than ten precious years with his children? It was too late by the time he realized his own response to this question.

This does not imply that working hard and having career aspirations are bad. In fact, I am in favor of both of these things. This story is meant to serve as yet another reminder of the importance of having the right goals and having the proper balance in your life. We only get one chance to live our lives. My former colleague had failed to define his goals properly. His overriding "make money so I can provide for my family" objective led him to extremes and distanced him from his family. He had incorrectly set his life compass, and it had placed him on the wrong path. I have personally known many others who, after reaching their goals, realized they weren't the right ones. Life is a one-way journey. We can't turn back the clock. My colleague won't get a second chance to adjust his past. The good news is that we can still determine our future. Before you start or continue your life journey, take some time to make sure you have defined the right goals for yourself. Make sure your compass is tuned properly and pointing in the right direction. What we do today and how we choose to spend our time, money, and energy should be consistent with achieving our goals.

Seize the Moment

You rarely get a second chance to relive an important moment. Trust your heart to dictate the right thing to do.

My father passed away in South Korea when I was in college at Virginia Tech. He was a wonderful, intelligent, generous, and hardworking man. Unfortunately, due to various family issues while I was young, I never got to know him very well. I grew up envious of friends who were close to their siblings and parents.

During high school and college, I had grand visions of being closer with my dad. He passed away before I could realize these visions. We never got to spend the time together that a father and son should. I never got to tell him that I loved him, despite my intention and several opportunities to do so. Saying a few words to another person shouldn't be very hard, but I chose to make it more difficult than it should have been. The expected momentary awkwardness and the deeply rooted Asian culture in me prevented me from ever telling him how I felt. Twenty years later, it remains one of the biggest regrets in my life. And it's one that I will never get a chance to change—at least not in this world. Don't procrastinate in doing what you know is right. Often, what we put off doesn't take much to accomplish. This is especially true when it comes to restoring relationships. Don't delay. Sooner or later, the opportunity will be taken away from you. Learn from my mistake and tell your loved ones how you feel. Even if you think they already know, tell them anyway. People desperately need and very much appreciate the assurance. I have now been married for more than a year. Every day, I make a point of telling my wife how beautiful she is (and I mean it). It has become a habit. She has yet to complain.

As a side note, don't underestimate the power of your words. Your words have the power to inspire, build, encourage, and heal, as well as to demotivate and destroy. It's easy to forget, misuse, or abuse this power. Choose your words carefully and wisely. A decade-long broken relationship may be restored with a few sincere and heartwarming words. Good intentions are worth very little if they remain mere intentions. Do it today.

Pursue Your Goals

I am proud to say that I thought of selling bottled water back in the late 1980s—years before it became so popular. I was convinced there was a huge market for it. There was never a doubt in my mind that people would pay a premium for a product that

*Plans are only good intentions
unless they immediately degenerate
into hard work.*
*—Peter Drucker, professor,
management consultant, and
prolific writer*

had traditionally been free. I was a visionary in this regard—along with perhaps a million others who had the same vision. Unfortunately, just like the vast majority of others, I only thought and dreamed of it. I never put my dreams into action. My conviction did not translate into success because I chose not to take any action.

On a much smaller scale, I have countless other "grand goals with no action" failure stories. I can go on and on, but here is one. When I first entered college, I was a fairly skinny, studious type, weighing just over 135 pounds. I really wanted to lose the nerdy image and be more athletic, mostly with the ultimate goal of being more popular with women. In my chemistry and basic engineering classes, I became friends with a guy from the Philippines, who was rather obese. Although we had two very different starting points, we had the same goal in mind: to get into better physical shape. We started lifting weights and playing basketball together, an extremely popular sport among Virginia Tech Hokies. By the end of our junior year, he was competing and winning body building contests and had transformed himself into a great ball player. I remained a casual weekend gym goer. The difference?

Simple—he took action to achieve his goal. For the first year, he would often call my dorm room to work out together early in the morning before classes. I found great excuses not to join him.

Having marvelous ideas, perfect plans, grand goals, honorable intentions, and daring dreams aren't good enough without action. If obstacles seem too great, break them down into smaller, manageable steps and take the first step. This is how you outswim your sharks. It's what separates winners from mere dreamers.

Would you want to be remembered as a person with grand plans and all the right intentions who took no action? Wake up and go after your dreams. Your dream can be as big as becoming a pioneer in a multibillion-dollar industry. It can be a personal goal to get in shape and be healthy. It can be to reconcile broken or damaged relationships with your family members or other loved ones. Regardless of your goal, the success depends on the actions you take.

Having goals is great, but you must go after them. The difference between success and failure is the willingness to put in the effort. You can't achieve anything worthwhile without the required effort. It's a simple yet valuable lesson I have learned personally over and over again. Just like any of life's simple truths, it is much easier said than done. Nevertheless, the choice is yours and yours alone.

CHAPTER 4
EXPECT TO PAY YOUR DUES IN FULL

Life grants nothing to us mortals without hard work.
—Horace, ancient Roman philosopher and poet

Setting aggressive goals and being motivated alone are not enough. There is no secret to outswimming your sharks. In their midst, you need to stay focused and passionate, working hard toward reaching your goals. Most people understand and agree with this simple truth. Yet very few people actually follow through. Choose to be among the few. Choose success.

You have a one in 3.8 million chance of winning a typical lottery where you select six out of a possible forty numbers. For the U.S. national lottery, the odds are significantly worse, with forty-nine numbers to choose from. With the additional nine numbers, the probability of winning is reduced to a meager one in 14 million. This, by the way, roughly equates to the probability of being struck by lightning twice in the same week. Pretty slim odds.

If we are after monetary peace of mind, it would be foolish to count on winning the lottery as a viable way to quickly reaching our financial success. Unfortunately, we live in a world of instant gratification. People usually do not have trouble setting lofty personal goals, but far too few are willing to work toward achieving them. This applies to career paths as well, whether you are an aspiring athlete or musician, scientist in search of a cure, teacher wishing to inspire young minds, entrepreneur contemplating your own business, or businessperson climbing the corporate ladder. Sadly, most people choose to succumb to the sharks in their lives. These sharks often become convenient excuses for their inaction and justifications for settling far below their full potential. Don't allow your sharks to get the better of you.

Hard Work

One should not expect to reap benefits without fully paying one's dues. There is one formula for success that's been proven effective over and over: hard work. I can't think of a single successful person who has not willingly worked diligently toward his or her goals. Achieving a meaningful accomplishment often takes perseverance in the face of major challenges.

Keep reminding yourself that success is a choice. Anyone can succeed—only a few are willing to put in the effort it takes. You can choose to win in your life. You can choose to be better at your profession. You can choose to mend broken relationships. You can choose to be a better spouse, parent, and friend. You can choose to live a healthier lifestyle. You can choose to conquer whatever shark species life has thrown at you. The choice to win needs to be complemented with appropriate actions and relentless pursuit. Are you ready to make the required payment to outswim your sharks?

> *Patience and perseverance have a magical effect before which difficulties disappear and obstacles vanish.*
> *—John Quincy Adams, sixth president of the United States*

Tiger Woods

Eldrick Tont Woods, better known as "Tiger" Woods, is arguably the best golfer of all time, having won an astonishing ninety-seven professional tournaments, seventy-one of those on the PGA Tour—all before the age of thirty-five. Woods held the number one position in the world rankings for the most consecutive weeks and for the greatest number of weeks. He has been awarded PGA Player of the Year ten times—yet another record. As of early 2011, his impressive winnings include four Masters Tournaments, four PGA Championships, three U.S. Open Championships, and three British Open Championships for a total of fourteen majors. In 2001, he became the first to hold all four professional major championships at the same time. He is the career victories leader among active players on the PGA Tour and is by far the leading money earner. In 2008 alone, he earned well over $100 million from winnings and endorsements, easily making him the highest-paid professional athlete in the world.

Despite his shortcomings as a married man, with a long history of infidelities that came to light in late 2009, there is little doubt that he will break all remaining meaningful golf records before he formally retires.

It seems there is no one who can match Tiger's physical prowess and his mental toughness. We are used to watching him on TV with his million-dollar endearing smile as he raises yet another trophy above his head. We hear stories about how he was already swinging a golf club when he was only nine months old, before he could walk. There are YouTube video clips of his appearance on *The Mike Douglas Show*, where he and Bob Hope had a putting contest when he was only three years old. Based on what we commonly read, hear, and see, we conclude that Tiger is a natural-born golfer, predestined for golf greatness. But is he? Was Tiger really predestined for golf greatness? Was he born with godlike golfing skills and abilities? I don't think this is the case.

In his most recent book, *Outliers: The Story of Success*, Malcolm Gladwell mentions case after case in which the key to one's success was the time devoted to a chosen field. This is the case in sports, computer programming, music, academics, and business. We don't usually see the painful preparation Tiger Woods voluntarily goes through on a constant basis. It's his daily devotion to golf that enabled him to remain the world's undisputed top golfer for so long. Yes, Tiger may be a naturally gifted golfer, but it's his work ethic that sets him apart. I read that Tiger gets up at dawn and often stays out on the course for as long as fourteen hours in a given day, hitting the little white balls again, again, again, and again in every conceivable situation in an attempt to reach perfection. He has paid and continues to pay his dues. This is a choice he makes every day. And the accumulation of his daily choices made it possible for him to become the greatest golfer of all time in his thirties.

Michael Phelps

Michael Phelps, also known as the "Baltimore Bullet" and "Human Dolphin," is an American swimmer. Since his spectacular and record-breaking performance at the 2008 Beijing Olympics, he is now hailed as the greatest Olympian of all time.

Phelps made his appearance on the world stage as the youngest member of the 2000 Sydney Olympic Games team. In Athens in 2004, his winning six gold and two bronze medals was one of the most amazing performances in Olympic swimming history—that is, of course, until the 2008 Beijing Olympics where he won eight gold medals, surpassing Mark Spitz's previous record of seven gold medals at the 1972 Munich Olympic Games. To put this in perspective, out of the eighty-one nations that competed in the 2008 Beijing Olympics, only four countries managed to win more gold medals than Michael Phelps—China, Russia, Great Britain, and the United States, whose total was largely thanks to Phelps.

I have read numerous articles in which the authors suggest that Phelps has a natural genetic advantage. Their arguments sound logical, considering his physical attributes: he has enormous feet (size 14) and a 6 foot 7 inch arm reach, which is significantly longer than his height of 6 feet 4 inches. His upper body, especially the shoulders, is much more developed than his legs, which gives him an additional advantage in the pool. His feet can rotate 15 degrees more than an average person's. His heart pumps 30 liters of blood each minute to his muscles, which is twice that of the average human. He also produces only one third of the lactic acid compared to the average swimmer, resulting in less muscle fatigue during intensive exercises. Taking these characteristics into account, the argument that Phelps is a natural swimmer begins to sound very convincing.

There is no doubt that Michael Phelps is extremely well suited to swimming. But is his success as a swimmer a mere result of some genetic lottery? Was he predestined to swimming greatness from the very start? Was he born with the perfect body for swimming?

I don't think this is the case. I actually find the argument a bit silly. Even if he does possess genetic advantages, I believe them to be secondary. Without focus, passion, and hard work, he would have likely turned out to be a mere above-average swimmer. There are a plethora of those types in this world. These are the people with God-given talents who choose not to exert themselves. I don't believe Phelps is a great swimmer due to his physical attributes. Rather, I believe his physical attributes are the results of his hard work. It's simply the case of his body responding to his lifestyle. When you swim extensively, your shoulders widen, lung capacity increases, etc. This is especially the case when you start intense training while you are young and your body is still growing. Michael Phelps started competing at age seven. His physical attributes, which many people consider unfair advantages, are direct results of his countless hours of grueling training in the water.

How long will you lie there, you sluggard? When will you get up from your sleep? A little sleep, a little slumber, a little folding of the hands to rest—and poverty will come on you like a bandit.
—Proverbs 6:9 and 10

The sacrifices Phelps voluntarily makes to attain his goals are enormous. Consider what Phelps chooses to go through to earn his medals: he trains in the water for six hours a day, six days a week, without exception. He consumes a staggering 12,000 calories each training day. To put this in perspective, an average adult only needs between 1,600 and 2,500 calories daily. I am willing to bet that any talented-enough athlete training hard enough to digest 12,000 calories per day will be on top of his or her game. Phelps's work ethic has made him a world champion. He worked for those medals and records. They weren't gifted to him genetically. Phelps has paid his dues in full.

These and all other champion athletes win their trophies and medals during their daily exhausting practices—through unbreakable focus, dedication, and unmatched hard work. Each day, they choose to win in their profession and back it up with the necessary hard work. The games merely serve as the official recognition ceremony of their daily choices.

Li Ka Shing

There are plenty of examples of personal success in other professions as well. Most people see the wealthy enjoying lifestyles they can only dream of. Few people realize what it took most of them to get there. Fewer still are willing to put in the necessary sacrifices and hard work like Li Ka Shing, the wealthiest man in

Asia, has done all of his life.

Li Ka Shing's empire includes Hutchison Whampoa and Cheung Kong Holdings, spans across ninety countries, accounts for over 10 percent of Hong Kong's stock market value, and controls well over 10 percent of all container port capacity in the world. He has achieved business and monetary success by any measure.

In order to become the financially successful Li Ka Shing that we know today, he had his own set of ferocious and uninvited sharks to conquer. At age twelve, Li Ka Shing fled with his family to Hong Kong as the Japanese invaded China. Upon his father's untimely death, he was forced to leave school to shoulder the responsibility of looking after his entire family, an immense burden for a fourteen-year-old child. Yet he did not cave in to these misfortunes. Even as a young child, he refused to surrender to his sharks. Li Ka Shing did not allow his tragedies to serve as excuses for settling for a life of poverty. Instead, he chose to stand his ground against his sharks and fight back.

In his early teenage years, young Li Ka Shing began his career by selling cheap watch bands in the narrow, dirty alleys and crowded markets in Hong Kong. Not exactly the glamorous image the world has of him today. He then moved up the ladder— selling plastic flowers. He routinely worked sixteen-hour days for many years just to barely survive and support his family. He continued to work relentlessly prior to starting his own first business in 1949 at the young age of twenty-one.

Sixty years later, in early 2010, Li Ka Shing's personal net worth was estimated at $21 billion, making him the fourteenth richest person on earth, according to *Forbes* magazine. He has certainly come a long way from his humble and most unlikely beginnings. He refused to succumb to his early tragedies and all the other sharks along the way. Against all odds, Li Ka Shing reached his financial success with pure determination and hard work. He didn't count on winning any lotteries.

He isn't embarrassed or resentful of his early life. In fact, Li Ka Shing credits it as a key to his success, perhaps even a necessity. It is doubtful whether he would have reached billionaire status had he been raised in a more secure, well-to-do family environment. It appears Li Ka Shing has not forgotten his lowly past. He is now one of the world's most generous philanthropists, having donated over $1.4 billion to date to charity and other philanthropic causes.

Most successful people have their own humble beginning story to share. What is common is that they fully and willingly paid their dues in sweat and hard work. For Li Ka Shing and many others, pure determination and hard work have paid off very well. It can and will happen for you as well. Whatever sharks you have in your life, you can outswim them all to attain success, but you must be ready to put in the hard work it will take. The choice to win in your life has always been, and will continue to be, yours and yours alone.

I could go on and on with examples. The point I'm emphasizing here is that hard work is mandatory and works without exception. It is my primary hope in writing this book to inspire you to work hard and relentlessly toward your worthwhile goals. Doing so is extremely difficult, and very few people choose to follow through. As you live your life, you shouldn't count on lucky breaks; chances are they will never come. Remember, you are more than twice as likely to die from a lightning strike than you are to win the lottery. Don't expect others to help you. Stop dreaming of your former bosses, colleagues, friends, or other acquaintances coming to your

Far and away the best prize that life offers is the chance to work hard at work worth doing.

—Theodore Roosevelt, twenty-sixth president of the United States

rescue. In this current time of economic uncertainty and high unemployment, don't expect the phone to ring with a job offer from one of these people. They are likely dealing with their own sharks. Don't expect them to protect you from yours.

You need sharks in order to become stronger and to reach your full potential. Consider your sharks as opportunities. Be grateful that you have them. The bigger the obstacle, the better the view will be once you climb on top of it. Learn to outswim your sharks on your own. If you are an athlete, don't succumb to the temptation to improve your performance by illegal means. Don't look for shortcuts in life. Instead, choose to work harder than your competition. If you are in the corporate world, don't play politics to get promoted. Work hard for your next step up. If it takes politics to get promoted, you're not in the right organization.

Don't be envious of others who have already succeeded. Life isn't necessarily about competing against others. Your achieving and living a successful life doesn't require someone else to fail. Rather, life is often about competing with ourselves, which requires fighting our natural tendencies and changing our bad habits.

Recommended Action

Get up early—each and every day. Perhaps we all deserve a lazy sleep-in day once in a while, but make a habit of starting your day early. I have yet to meet anyone who has succeeded in his or her field who doesn't get up early. During my twenty-year corporate career, I have known and worked with more than a hundred C-level executives. If there is one common trait they all have, it is that they start their days early. The vast majority of them get up at 6 AM or earlier. This trait is true regardless of industry, educational background, geographic location, age, etc. We simply can't achieve much in life by being lazy. As the Bible states in Proverbs 20:13, "Do not love sleep or you will grow poor."

It isn't easy swimming with the sharks. Just as true, there is no secret to outswimming them. You can create a success story of your own. First, you need to set the right goals for yourself, ones that are consistent with how you ultimately want to be remembered and that will positively impact the lives of those you love. Once you have those goals, don't give up. Focus on what you can directly control—how you choose to spend today and this very moment. Outswim your sharks with unwavering determination and hard work. Expect and be prepared to pay your dues in full.

• CHAPTER 5

KEEP YOUR CHARACTER AND INTEGRITY

Character, in the long run, is the decisive factor in the
life of an individual and of nations alike.

—*Theodore Roosevelt, twenty-sixth president of the United States*

You are more than your title at work or the clothes you wear. Your salary or net worth does not equate to your value as an individual. Regardless of what others may have you believe, your character counts more than your assets. You will at some point undoubtedly be tempted to compromise your character for a gain. Don't take the bite. Stand firm against such lures. Nothing can possibly be worth losing your integrity.

Many people choose the easy way. We see examples of this everywhere: a student cheating on an exam, a sports figure taking steroids or other illegal substances to improve his performance, a con artist taking innocent people's hard-earned money. Watching news reports about these kinds of people on TV, I sometimes get the sense they are more ashamed and regretful that they have been caught than they are for their dishonorable actions.

A good name is more desirable than great riches.
—Proverbs 22:1

A TV broadcaster described one such individual, a famous major league baseball player, as a "fallen hero." I disagreed with his word choice. He was not a fallen hero; he was a false hero.

Don't ever jeopardize your reputation. A medal gained by bending the rules is worthless and often rightfully taken away from the athlete.

There are less extreme examples. A job applicant who makes a false claim on her resume can never fully regain her integrity and respect. A few extra dollars gained from adding false claims to an expense report will not equal the integrity that is lost. A dubious deduction on a tax return, which may raise questions about your character, is to be avoided at all costs. Character and integrity supersede all professional and financial gains.

I was once tempted to short-sell a particular stock for a quick and easy profit. The idea came to me during a casual dinner with several other senior leadership members, which involved many bottles of wine and other forms of alcohol. Our CEO made a few comments concerning his personal friends who held various C-level positions at another firm in a completely different industry. This was a rather large, publicly traded firm, and I knew the firm's stock price would free-fall when the news concerning a major accounting adjustment for uncollectible debt became public. It was a piece of information I never asked for—one that I could have used to make quick returns. For most of us, it's difficult to turn down free money. I struggled quite a bit for the next few days before finally coming to my senses and deciding that the fast cash was not worth risking my integrity. Sure enough, on the day of the news less than two weeks later, the stock lost over 40 percent in value in just a matter of hours. Funny, but I actually felt good about my decision.

As human beings, we are given the amazing ability to reason. Unfortunately, we sometimes misuse this gift to justify just about anything: "Everyone does it." "I'm not hurting anyone." I have used these and other similar justifications myself many times. These are poor and unacceptable excuses—nothing is worth more than a clear conscience. It's never too late. We can start today.

Retain Integrity as You Move Up

After more than twenty years at a research/analysis organization in Washington DC, Paul Feldman left a comfortable senior-level position and a good salary to deliver bagels. Yes, bagels. His business model couldn't have been simpler. In the morning, he delivered fresh bagels to various locations in the Washington DC area, and in the afternoon he returned to collect the cash payment. In just a few years, Feldman was selling more than 8,000 bagels each week to 140 organizations. This, by the way, allowed him to earn just as much as before. Feldman's simple business model required an "honor" payment system. Next to his bagels, Feldman left a cash basket where people made their payment. With more than two decades of analytical background, Feldman naturally kept track of all data—the money collected vs. bagels consumed at each of his locations. He was therefore able to tell down to the penny how honest each of his 140 customers were. He also started measuring other major variables that played into the collection probability. These included size of offices (smaller offices are more honest), weather (cold, heavy rain, or wind makes people less honest), types of holidays (people are more honest during the Fourth of July, Labor Day, and Columbus Day weeks, whereas Valentine's Day, Thanksgiving, and Christmas weeks have the opposite effect, perhaps due to monetary spending involved and high expectations from loved ones). Other interesting findings? Feldman also concluded, after delivering for many years to a particular company spread over multiple floors (with executives on the top floor), that people further up the corporate ladder cheat more than those below (perhaps due to a sense of entitlement).

As you proceed through life, keep your integrity and character intact. After all, you don't want to get to the top of your particular ladder by compromising your morals. And it doesn't have to be something as extensive as WorldCom, Enron, or the Madoff scandal to ruin your reputation. As you move up within your organization, be sure to set a good example. No matter how people may try to persuade you, make no compromises when it comes to your personal character or integrity. This applies regardless of your profession—whether business, law, sports, entertainment, whatever. Protect your character and integrity. Once tainted, they can rarely be fully regained. Live an honest life. You will feel a lot better when you succeed fairly.

PART II

SWIMMING WITH THE SHARKS

CHAPTER 6

WHAT HAVE YOU BEEN DOING LATELY?

For those to whom much is given, much is required.
—*John F. Kennedy, thirty-fifth president of the United States*

Your today is an accumulated result of your yesterdays—the planned and unplanned events that took place in your life, decisions you made, people you met and chose to associate with, actions you took, ways you chose to invest your time, money, and effort. In the same way, how you spend today will shape your tomorrow.

A worthy goal is not easily or instantly achieved. For someone wishing to lose weight and get in better shape, a strict diet demands more than a single healthy meal. The greatest workout program is of little value unless it is practiced over and over again. Nor does being a great athlete or musician happen overnight. The principle remains the same in the business environment. Sales won't increase without persistent effort to win customers over again and again. Turning around an organization takes passion, leadership, and hard work over many weeks, months, and perhaps years. Developing meaningful and lasting relationships with your spouse, children, and other loved ones takes much patience, understanding, and constant nurturing. Being recently married, I am personally learning this lesson.

We live in a world of instant gratification. People dream of success, but many are unwilling to pay the price for it. Given focus and passion, time and sweat are the two common currencies you can use to pay for meaningful success. What have you been doing lately? Where will that lead you? Have you defined the right goals for yourself? Have you taken into account what's truly important in your life in setting those goals? Are you acting consistently in achieving those goals? Or have you allowed your sharks to become excuses for inaction?

Don't Allow Your Shoulds to Become Excuses

You can choose to get on your own path to success at any time. I highly recommend that you start today. After all, today is the first day of the rest of your life. To reach your goals, you don't necessarily have to know all the answers in advance. The answers will come in due time. You need to take the first step in order to see the next step. If one of your goals is to lose twenty pounds, don't delay shedding the first pound because you are busy developing the perfect plan to lose the last pound. Don't worry so much about what lies dimly at a distance. Instead, focus and take action on what lies clearly ahead. If you focus too much on potential problems, you will fail to see the potential solutions.

Are you allowing your sharks to get the better of you while you choose to stand still? Are you acting consistently with how you ultimately want to be remembered? If you continue on your current path, where will you end up? If needed, make the proper adjustments today to get back on the right path. You are accountable for what you choose to do, what you choose not to do, and what you make out of your life. Don't allow your sharks to become convenient excuses for failure.

There is no need to fear or swim away from your sharks. Don't shy away when faced with what appears to be an insurmountable problem. Break it into parts and handle them one at a time. It's the project you continually hesitate to start that takes the longest to complete. The best and also the fastest way to jump-start the rest of your life is to start immediately. You are bigger and stronger than any of the sharks allowed in your life.

There may have been major unexpected events in your past. There will continue to be challenges that are completely out of your immediate control. You may not have had any say in these sharks entering your life, but you have full control over how you respond to them. All of us, without exception, are where we are as a consequence of our past, and our future is being formed by how we choose to spend this very moment. Do your actions today align with how you want to be remembered tomorrow? What have you been doing lately? Where will that lead you?

CHAPTER 7

DON'T ASK FOR A SHARK-FREE LIFE

If you find a path with no obstacles, it probably doesn't lead anywhere.
—Frank A. Clark, newspaper columnist who created "The Country Parson,"
popular one-panel cartoons from the mid-1950s to early 1980s

There will always be sharks in our lives. We shouldn't be afraid of or shy away from them. They are put in our lives for us to conquer and enable us to become stronger.

You have been given life. You are now the sole owner of this great gift. You and you alone are accountable for what you make of this marvelous gift from our Maker. Choose to take control and make things happen in your life rather than letting things happen to you. In the words of Irene C. Kassorla, psychologist and author, "You must have control of the authorship of your own destiny. The pen that writes your life story must be held in your own hand." Each of us has a story, and we play the main character in that story. We write the plot as we live our lives.

Do you want your life story to be one without a clear plot, direction, or purpose? You have a choice on what to make out of your life. It's up to you to create and live a masterpiece that will inspire others.

You are bigger and stronger than the sharks allowed in your life. Take control of and responsibility for your own life.

You don't want a trouble-free life. Be thankful for the sharks in your life. There are none, no matter how big they appear to be, that you cannot outswim. If God has allowed them in your life, He knows you are capable of outswimming them. There is a Bible verse in the book of I Corinthians that reads "God is faithful. He will not allow problems beyond what you can handle." This is a promise from our Maker. It has served as a much-needed source of comfort and reassurance many times in my life.

Abraham Lincoln

Born in a small wood cabin to a poor and illiterate farmer. Less than one year of formal education. Went into business with a friend early in life and found himself in bankruptcy upon the friend's death. Spent the next half decade working to completely pay off his deceased friend's debt.

This may not sound like the bio of anyone who has attained any level of significance. But in fact it is. It is the very humble beginning of the sixteenth president of the United States, Abraham Lincoln. He happens to be one of my favorite leaders of all time. More books have been written about Abraham Lincoln than any other American. In the book *Team of Rivals* by Pulitzer Prize–winning historian Doris Kearns Goodwin, Leo Tolstoy, the brilliant Russian historian and author, is quoted to have said the following about Lincoln: "The greatness of Napoleon, Caesar, or Washington is only moonlight by the sun of Lincoln. His example is universal and will last thousands of years. . . . He was bigger than his country—bigger than all the presidents all together . . . and as a great character he will live as long as the world lives." John Hay, who served as Lincoln's personal assistant in the White House and later as secretary of state for two other presidents, called Lincoln "the greatest character since Christ."

How did Lincoln become such an influential figure? Without a formal education, who taught him how to lead an entire nation through one of its most turbulent times? What made Lincoln who he was?

Lincoln certainly had his share of sharks in his life, before and even after he became president. Consider the following difficulties, challenges, naysayers, and less-than-favorable circumstances he had to deal with:

- Lincoln's mother died when he was still a child.

- Without any financial means, he had to study on his own to become a lawyer.

- Throughout his political career, Lincoln was often humiliated by the press and was referred to as a grotesque baboon, an ape, a third-rate country lawyer splitting the Union, and a dictator. In his home state, the *Illinois State Register* labeled him "the craftiest and most dishonest politician that ever disgraced an office in America."

- In 1858, Lincoln lost the Illinois state senate race to Stephen A. Douglas due to his stance on slavery. Lincoln knew very well that his antislavery belief could cost him the election, but he refused to back down or compromise.

- Lincoln was elected president by a minority of the popular vote and was seen by his own advisers as nothing more than a gawky, incompetent country lawyer with no leadership experience.

- Ten days before Abraham Lincoln took the oath of office in 1861, the Confederate States of America separated from the Union, taking all Federal agencies, forts, and arsenals within their territory.

- In her nearly 800-page book *Team of Rivals*, author Doris Kearns Goodwin claims, "Every member of his administration was better known, better educated, and more experienced in public life than Lincoln."

- After being elected president, he had to borrow money for his train ticket to Washington DC to give his acceptance speech.

Despite all the odds stacked against him, in the midst of all his sharks, Lincoln established himself as the epitome of integrity and remained committed to his morals. Without any formal education or professional training, Lincoln also transformed himself into one of the greatest motivational speakers. It is well known that Lincoln wrote his own speeches, many of which are today regarded as masterpieces of poetic and artistic expression.

Lincoln's ability to bring out the best in other people is legendary. This was especially evident in how he dealt with those he worked with in the White House. Many of them had contested his running for presidency, and just about all of them considered themselves superior in intellect, ability, and appearance. Even for Lincoln, I imagine it had to be pretty difficult at first being a leader with so many unwilling followers.

Because they had been political adversaries and harsh critics, Lincoln could have shut them out after winning the presidency and becoming, essentially, their boss. That's what most people expected and exactly what most politicians do. Lincoln, however, did just the opposite. He recognized each individual's unique talents and knew each person had something of value to offer. He successfully united his former rivals and initially unwilling followers. Lincoln was able to create a common and unwavering goal required to get through one of the greatest crises to face the nation—the Civil War. As Goodwin writes, Lincoln succeeded "through his extraordinary array of personal qualities that enabled him to form friendships with men who had previously opposed him; to repair injured feelings that, left untended, might have escalated

Stand up to your obstacles and do something about them. You will find that they haven't half the strength you think they have.
—Norman Vincent Peale, Protestant preacher and author of The Power of Positive Thinking

into permanent hostility; to assume responsibility for the failures of subordinates; to share credit with ease; and to learn from mistakes."

Would we know the name Abraham Lincoln, the great man we admire and respect today, had he lived a shark-free life? Had Lincoln been born to a wealthy, stable family, would he have been able to become president and free the slaves? Had he attended and graduated

The strongest oak tree of the forest is not the one that is protected from the storm and hidden from the sun. It's the one that stands in the open where it is compelled to struggle for its existence against the winds and rains and the scorching sun.

—Napoleon Hill, American self-improvement author

from an established institution with the right personal connections, would he have run for and won the presidency? We will never know the answers to these hypothetical questions. I wonder how the world would have turned out had another person been elected sixteenth president of the United States.

Lincoln's problems, circumstances, and other species of sharks were instrumental in forming his character and helping him realize his true potential as a leader. Lincoln became the person we know today by conquering his sharks.

Struggles Are Often Needed to Fulfill One's Destiny

A man found a cocoon containing a caterpillar, soon to be a butterfly. As expected, a small opening appeared at the tip of the cocoon one day. The man observed the butterfly intently for several hours as it struggled to force its body through this tiny gap. After a while, it seemed to stop making any progress, as if it had gotten as far as it could on its own. With noble intent, the man decided to assist this little, helpless creature. He took a pair of scissors and snipped off the remaining bit of the cocoon. The butterfly was then able to emerge easily out of its cocoon. But it had a swollen body, still resembling that of a caterpillar, and small, shriveled, underdeveloped wings.

The man continued to watch the butterfly because he expected its body to eventually get smaller. He expected the wings to eventually enlarge and expand. To his disappointment, neither happened. The butterfly spent the rest of its life crawling around with a swollen body and shriveled wings. It never flew. It never fully became a butterfly with large, beautiful wings, as it was meant to be.

What the man in his kindness and haste did not understand was that the confining cocoon and the struggle required for the butterfly to get through the tiny opening were nature's way of forcing fluid from the body of the butterfly into its wings so it would be ready for flight once it achieved its freedom from the cocoon.

Sometimes struggles are exactly what we need in our lives. If we go through our lives avoiding obstacles, we will never reach our full potential. Just as struggles were necessary to transform a ground-crawling cat-erpillar into a butterfly with beautiful wings, problems and hard times help us complete our own metamorphosis into a better being.

> *The gem cannot be polished without friction, nor man perfected without trials.*
> —*Chinese proverb*

By definition, hard times are not pleasant to go through. Keep fighting and envision yourself out of the cocoon. In the words of Sir Winston Churchill, "When going through hell, keep going."

Welcome the Challenge

Just as the man in the preceding story had the right intentions but ultimately caused a detrimental ending for the butterfly, there will be people in our lives who will cause us harm despite their gracious and noble intent.

If you are out of college, don't make a habit of relying on your parents for financial support. Learn to live within your means and to stand on your own. If you are after a promotion or a pay raise at work, work for it. Work harder than your peers to get it. Avoid playing the office politics and don't kiss up. Yes, there will be people who move up the ladder this way. I have seen plenty of these types myself. Choose not to be one. Earn your way up. If you are a musician, don't rely on your connections to land you a spot in the orchestra. Practice to hone your skills so that you will be the logical choice. If you are an athlete, work hard to land the starting position. Don't succumb to the temptation to take the shortcut. People who generously offer you shortcuts aren't interested in your long-term well-being.

Be careful and think twice before you accept help from others. By accepting someone else's help or by taking a shortcut, you may be clipping your own wings. Yes, you will be able to put an end to the immediate struggle and crawl out of the cocoon, but keep in mind, there is a good reason for your struggles. You need to overcome them before you can fly.

Obstacles will look large or small to you according to whether you are large or small.
—Orison Swett Marden, American writer

The sharks are required for you to fly and to realize your full potential. Be happy for the problems you have in life. The bigger they are, the stronger you will be once you triumph over them.

The Story of Joseph

Although they may be unclear at first, choose to believe there are reasons for your sufferings rather than succumbing to them. In the Bible, Joseph is betrayed and sold by his brothers at a young age. He first ends up as a slave in Egypt. I wonder how bitter he was toward his family and the fate life had dealt him. But funny enough, there is no mention of Joseph ever being discouraged or resentful about what happened to

Who has never tasted what is bitter does not know what is sweet.

—German proverb

him. Instead, he works hard to "win the favor of his master." Just as things finally seem to be getting better for Joseph, he is falsely accused of wrongdoing and is unjustly sent to prison where he spends most of his prime years. He helps one of his cellmates, who immediately fails to remember his favor. What a wasted life, one may conclude. Fortunately, the story does not end there.

In the end, we realize that what appeared at first to be a series of disastrous and unfair events was necessary to achieve something much greater. The sharks in Joseph's life eventually led him to climb the political ladder in Egypt. Without his shrewdness and wise decisions as the second in command in Egypt, millions would have died of hunger, including his own family. The betrayal by his brothers, the slavery, and the unjust imprisonment were what he needed to overcome to achieve his historic accomplishment.

There are reasons for the sharks in your life. A shark-free life is boring and not worth living. Sharks have been allowed in your life so you may conquer them. There is a better you waiting on the other side. Sharks represent opportunities to develop and showcase your full potential. What appears to be disastrous and unfair may very well be what you need to overcome to enrich your own life and those of others. Learn to accept the sharks in your life. Learn to appreciate them. They are there for you to conquer. Don't ask for a shark-free life.

CHAPTER 8

MASTER YOUR CHOSEN FIELD

Make the most of yourself, for that is all there is of you.
—Ralph Waldo Emerson, American essayist, philosopher, and poet

For a handful of years, I worked out of mid-Manhattan on the corner of 49th Street and 3rd Avenue. One of the best things about living in or visiting a metropolitan area is the diversity and wide range of great food it offers. This is a big plus if you happen to be a food lover like me.

Based on a wild guess by a close former associate of mine, there are well over two thousand restaurants in Manhattan and its surrounding boroughs. Although I cannot validate the absolute accuracy of this count, I do trust that it is in the ballpark since he is one of those people who seems to know everything about any topic. He also happens to be a fellow food lover, so there is at least some level of credibility to his estimate.

Despite the overwhelming number of restaurants in the city that never sleeps, there are only a dozen or so that I truly enjoy and actually look forward to visiting. I am certain that even if I were to try every single one of the city's restaurants, my list would extend to only fifty at most. So, what do I make of the other two thousand restaurants? Not much, I am afraid.

Unfortunately, there are plenty of examples like this in life. Having spent many years of my life in several universities (too embarrassing to admit the number), I have studied under approximately a hundred professors. However, there are only three whom I regard as great teachers. These individuals have significantly influenced my life, and I actually remember what they taught me.

There are similar examples in all aspects of life. There may be dozens or perhaps hundreds of people you associate with at work. But if you were to start a company of your own, how many of these bosses, peers, and subordinates would you want to take with you? Consider the flip side. If any of these people were to start their own company, how many of them would consider you to be the "must-have" person? Have you reached your personal best at what you do? Just as it is easy to put up a sign outside a restaurant that reads "Joe's Pizza—City's Best," it is easy to claim being the best at whatever you do. But do others recognize you as such? Do people see you making the honest and maximum effort in your life? Have you put in your dues to excel in your chosen field? Or, heaven forbid, are you looking for shortcuts in life?

Time is the coin of your life. It is the only coin you have, and only you can determine how it will be spent. Be careful lest you let other people spend it for you.
—Carl Sandburg, American poet and writer

There are lots and lots of opportunities out there. Choose your field wisely and give it your best shot. There is no room for half-hearted effort—it will get you nowhere in life. With a mere average effort, you will end up—you guessed it—average. There is nothing wrong with this, but if you want to rise to the top, you must be willing to sacrifice more than others.

Are you hesitating to go into a particular field because of expected competition? There may be many in your profession, but remember, most of the competition is mediocre. There are only a few worthy competitors in life. You can devote yourself to being one of them.

With a Strong Enough Will, You Will Find a Way

You don't think there is enough time? It's all about prioritizing—knowing what's most important to you and making up your mind to do it. Let me share just one example.

While living in Sweden, I met a woman at work who spoke almost fluent English without a formal education. She mastered the language in less than three years by studying daily on her own, watching American movies over and over, and reading books and listening to audio books on the bus or subway on her way to and from work. Her spoken and written English skills were far better than most of the upper managers, many of whom had graduated from top European universities.

Where there is a strong enough will, there is a way. Make the time and effort toward your worthwhile goals. Don't let lack of formal education or any other sharks in your life discourage you from pursuing your goals.

Whatever professional career path you choose, you can be an expert at what you do. Devote an extra thirty minutes each day to mastering your field. It may require extra reading, writing, phone calls, practice, etc. The additional half hour will make you an expert in only a couple of years.

CHAPTER 9
DEVELOP AN UNBREAKABLE
FOCUS AND MOTIVATION

Success is the ability to go from one failure to another with no loss of enthusiasm.
—Sir Winston Churchill, British politician best known for
his leadership during World War II

Do you have a problem focusing and concentrating? Or is your lack of focus an inevitable consequence of not having a goal? It's hard to focus when you don't have clear goals. The concept is no different from having a definite destination in mind before you start driving. You should have a clear picture of where you want your life journey to take you and focus on how to reach that destination.

Or perhaps you have too many goals? Quantity is not a good substitute for quality. To succeed, you need to be extremely selective in what you want out of life. You will achieve the most by focusing on one thing at a time. This means making sure the project scope and objectives do not get out of hand. If your goal is to be a professional athlete, it means finding the one sport to focus on. If you are an aspiring musician, it means choosing the one instrument to master. If you are a lawyer, it means selecting a specific field to excel in. If you are an artist, it means defining your own style and medium. You can expand and become more versatile later if you wish, but start by focusing on one thing at a time.

Reprogramming

We human beings have a tendency to imagine the worst. We are born with it, and it remains with us until we recognize it and consciously reprogram ourselves. This reprogramming is essential in keeping ourselves focused and motivated.

A sleepy child, when disturbed by the thought of monsters under the bed, will suddenly awaken. Trust me on this—I speak from experience. When the lights go out, the child will become too scared to fall asleep as his or her childlike imagination runs wild. Adults aren't much better at times. Someone once defined adulthood as repressed childhood. I thought it was funny at the time, but I think there is a lot of truth in that statement. Over the years, we have mastered the art of concealing our emotions. We have learned to conform to the norms of our society. But deep inside, the fragile child in us remains. We still possess the need to be loved, appreciated, and accepted by others. For many of us, our deeply rooted tendency of imagining the worst has become a habit. We fear rejection and failure prior to even trying. Before we make the phone call, we imagine the person on the other end of the line saying no, or worse, hanging up on us. We imagine our client deciding to go with another agency as we prepare for the final presentation. We imagine ourselves falling short of contractual requirements. We imagine our contracts not being renewed. We imagine our bosses and/or peers laughing at our ideas. We imagine our competition outperforming us. We imagine and waste way too much time on things going wrong. If you have this tendency, it is one of the major sharks in your life that you will need to conquer before you can reach success.

Having a backup plan in case things don't go as we planned is a prudent approach. But don't dwell too much on what can go wrong. Sooner or later, your pessimistic imaginings will become expectations, and your gloomy expectations will define and shape your attitude and your approach to life. Learn to replace your fear of potential failure with the expectation of deserved success, as long as you are willing to devote the time and put in the necessary hard work. This is how we start reprogramming against our natural pessimistic tendencies. Choose to imagine the best scenario, appropriate to the dedication and hard work you are putting in. Imagine the wonderful feeling of reaching your goals. Vividly visualize yourself on top of the obstacle that at first seemed insurmountable. Think, imagine, and expect success. This is how you keep yourself motivated to work even harder toward your goals.

Maintaining Focus and Motivation

Assuming you have defined the right goals for yourself and have not overburdened yourself with too many goals, here are some practical points I use to help maintain my focus and motivation.

He that can't endure the bad, will not live to see the good.
—Jewish proverb

Long-term goals may seem abstract and out of reach when starting out. It is often difficult to stay focused on goals that take weeks, months, or perhaps years to achieve. I find breaking down long-term goals into a short-term to-do list helps. Translate this into a list of clear actions you can take daily to work toward the goal. This concrete list of actions will help you stay on track. At an absolute minimum, work with a weekly to-do list.

Refer to your short- and long-term lists often. I read my lists multiple times each day. I realize this sounds elementary, but I have found this process to be quite helpful. I know several others, whom I regard as extremely successful in their own chosen fields, who practice the same habit. The old Chinese proverb "The palest ink is better than the best memory" contains wisdom gained over many centuries. With each passing year, as my memory fades, I find myself agreeing more and more with this proverb. Write your to-do lists. Refer to them regularly. Prioritize and work on the toughest tasks first; your day will get easier as the end nears.

At a bare minimum, review your daily to-do list each night (the goal is to have all the items crossed off), and create a new one for the next day. Your mind is still active while you sleep. Put it to good use—give it something to reflect on overnight. Each morning, you should also begin the day by reviewing the to-do items you have written the night before. Once writing daily to-do lists becomes a habit, start creating weekly and monthly versions with the highest priority items at the top of your list. Make sure there is a clear connection between your long-term goal and the items on your to-do list.

Visualize, Visualize, Visualize

Visualize the sweet success and the ultimate realization of your goals. It's the moment everyone at work celebrates your project's huge success. It's the moment when you proudly lift the trophy over your head. It's the moment you cross the finish line ahead of the other runners. It's the moment you open the acceptance letter from your dream school. It's the moment the lone spotlight is pointed on you and your piano in the darkened concert hall. It's the moment your name is called at an award ceremony and the crowd breaks into a well-deserved standing ovation. Whatever your chosen field, clearly visualize the defining moment. For me, it's the image of seeing people reading my books, translated into different languages, at random places (on planes and trains, in coffee shops, etc.) around the world.

In becoming one of the greatest golfers of all time, Jack Nicklaus relied on a visualization technique described in his book *Golf My Way*:

> I never hit a shot, even in practice, without having a very sharp, in-focus picture of it in my head. It's like a color movie. First, I "see" the ball where I want it to finish, nice and white and sitting up high on the bright green grass. Then the scene quickly changes and I "see" the ball going there: its path, trajectory, and shape, even its behavior on landing. Then there's a sort of fade-out, and the next scene shows me making the kind of swing that will turn the previous image into reality.

This visualization technique is extremely common among successful people. Start imagining and visualizing yourself achieving your goals and reaching success. Use this positive image to motivate yourself to work harder.

I should point out that this visualization technique is intended to help you focus and motivate you toward your goal. Avoid going to extremes. If you find yourself daydreaming and it is hindering you from focusing and getting things done, you have gone too far.

Take a Break Once in a While

You can't expect to go on a thousand-mile journey without ever refueling your gas tank. Reenergize by doing something you really enjoy. Finally do the very thing you have been meaning and wanting to do. Reward yourself for the diligent effort and accomplishments to date. If your goal is to lose fifty pounds, stop to celebrate with a small scoop of ice cream each time you lose ten pounds. Remember to keep your ultimate goal in mind and resist the temptation to go back to your old ways.

Celebrate with your team members and people you enjoy being with. After all, life is meant to be enjoyed and shared with others. Visit a friend. Surprise your spouse by planning a nice romantic dinner at home. Attend a cooking session with your spouse. Go biking with your child. Take a leisurely drive to the beach or the mountains. Spend a day volunteering at a homeless shelter. Once in a while, get away from what you are doing. If you are leading a team toward a common goal, take the team out to a nice casual dinner and drinks. If you are an athlete, take a day off from hard training; your muscles will thank you for it. Let it serve as motivation to work out even harder the next day. If you are a professor or a researcher, take some time off to read about a topic that is completely foreign to you. Once again, avoid going to extremes and resorting to old habits. Life is all about proper balance. These breaks should serve as rejuvenation and small celebrations along the way toward your ultimate goals.

Come Up with Your Own Success Story

Focus and motivation are necessary for hard work. They are also the main raw ingredients for success. The key to getting a lot done in your life is to give your best on the single task you are working on at any moment.

There is no time to be jealous of others, so don't let someone else's success distract you. There is little value in debating whether your peer deserves a promotion, an award, recognition, or whatever. Don't allow jealousy to become a shark that diverts you from focusing on your goals. We already have enough sharks in our lives; there is no need to create more. Choose to focus on what you can directly control—how you spend your own time and effort. Be happy for others who succeed and come up with your own success story.

Recommended Activities

To help you maintain your focus and motivation, use the following four guiding points discussed in this chapter:

1. Translate your long-term goals into clear short-term to-do lists (preferably daily).

2. Write and habitually review these goals and to-do items.

3. Visualize the moment of achieving your long-term goal.

4. Celebrate the progress and achievements along the way.

CHAPTER 10
REVIEW YOUR GOALS

To keep a lamp burning we have to keep putting oil in it.

—Mother Teresa

Have you set your goals? What are they for this year? For this week? For today? Are they consistent with how you want to be remembered? Regularly reflect on your goals to make sure they are right for you now and in the future. Remember, you will not reach your intended destination if your life compass is pointing in the wrong direction. Don't let any of your many sharks distract you from pursuing and reaching your goals.

Once you have a clear set of goals, develop a habit of reviewing and evaluating them to make sure they are the right ones. After all, you don't want to get to the top of the ladder only to realize it's the wrong one.

Everyone is given twenty-four hours a day. This is true regardless of age, gender, social status, educational background, and any other arbitrary classification we can come up with. Yet some people manage to achieve so much more in their lives than others. How do you achieve more in a fixed, equal amount of time? Forming worthwhile goals and regularly evaluating progress are the first steps.

A 1,000 mile journey begins with the first step. In setting goals, be specific and break them down into smaller components you can track on a daily and weekly basis. On a day-to-day and on a weekly basis, develop a habit of making to-do lists. Make a list of your goals and carry it with you at all times. I find this extremely helpful in keeping track of my priorities. I write my daily and weekly goals on a small piece of paper, and I carry it with me in my wallet as a constant reminder of what I need to do. I cross tasks off as I complete them. For monthly and annual goals, I track them on an Excel spreadsheet. It may sound trivial and insignificant, but this approach is quite helpful for me. Since I have started using it, I find myself wasting less time.

I once drove from Cardiff, Wales, to a friend's home in London, England, a distance of approximately 130 miles. This was in the mid-1990s before GPS devices became ubiquitous in rental cars. Many of the roads in the United Kingdom are small and difficult to follow unless you are familiar with the area. Luckily, I had a good old-fashioned map with me, and I found myself referring to it quite often to make sure I was on the right path.

> *Review your goals twice every day in order to be focused on achieving them.*
> *—Les Brown, Motivational speaker*

Even with the map, I made a few wrong turns along the way and had to make some unintended trip modifications. Although this weekend journey took a mere two and a half hours, it would have been extremely difficult without the clear road map and the constant review of it. Let your goals serve as the road map of your life. Your daily, weekly, and monthly tasks are the turns and decisions you must make to stay on course. Regular review of your goals and tasks is an absolute necessity in reaching your final destination.

Once a year, usually in late December or early January, I try to spend one full day alone, without any interruptions, to reflect on the prior year and to plan for the future. For those of you in the corporate world, this is similar in nature to the annual performance reviews. Spending some quiet time by yourself can be extremely valuable in setting or, when needed, resetting your life compass. While I lived in Hong Kong, I used to take a long hike on the Diamondback trail. In the United States, I would drive several hours each way to make a quick visit with a friend whom I didn't get to see very often. During my short stint in Europe, I would find a nice quiet café (surprisingly, there aren't as many as you might think) and spend most of one day there to reflect on the past twelve months and set goals for the upcoming year.

Regularly review your goals. Are they the right ones? Are you making progress? Setting the right goals and habitually review-ing them will help you fight off shark attacks. When a new shark emerges in your life, make sure to review your ultimate goals in order to deal with it correctly.

At least once a year, find your own place of comfort and spend time with yourself to reflect, evaluate, and plan. Use this unin-terrupted time to make sure you are headed in the right direction in your life and to gauge your progress toward your life goals. It may be the most valuable day of your year.

PART III

OVERCOMING SHARK ATTACKS

CHAPTER 11

TREAT PEOPLE WITH RESPECT AND DIGNITY

The true measure of a man is how he treats someone
who can do him absolutely no good.
—*Samuel Johnson, English author, poet, essayist, moralist,*
novelist, and biographer

Life is not a game of predator and prey. Succeeding in life does not require someone else to lose. Deal with everyone equally. Treat people with respect and dignity. This applies to those above you, below you, and everywhere in between.

Be Nice

I once had a longtime peer at work who was eventually promoted and became my boss. It was awkward at first, but I had no issues with the situation, as I had much respect and admiration for this individual. The fact that he was more than ten years my senior also helped ease me into the new relationship. I was quite happy for him. In fact, most of his former peers, newly made direct reports, were happy for him. He was exceptionally capable and worked well with others. During his time as our peer, he had earned our respect. His previous subordinates also had plenty of positive things to say about him. He was a perfect gentleman— and I often find myself wanting to adopt his style of dealing with people. He was a great individual to work with as a peer who rightfully became a leader with many willing followers.

Unfortunately, I have also known, and even worked closely with, people on the other extreme of the spectrum. They are unpleasant to be around, and most people simply put up with them because they have no other short-term choice. I just hope I am not one of these people to someone else. As the old saying goes, "Everybody is somebody's difficult person." Perhaps I should learn to serve as the designated difficult person to the difficult people of this world.

Some people believe that to succeed in life, especially in their chosen professional field, they can't be too nice. While working in the automotive industry, I once had a colleague who considered it perfectly okay to backstab his peers to move up the ranks. He openly and frequently spoke about this belief and many other personal views and philosophies that were just as much rubbish. In his opinion, business and personal matters were completely separate, with an entirely different set of moral standards. His behavior toward others at work, he warned, should not be taken personally. He personified the stereotypical human version of a shark.

Sadly, I know many others with similar views and behaviors. They argue that being nice should be reserved for family and personal friends. They believe that being nice will be considered a weakness in the harsh, cut-throat business world. After twenty years of climbing the corporate ladder, I found this common belief to be incorrect. You can be nice, firm, and effective at the same time. Don't let anyone fool you into believing otherwise. Don't let the human sharks in your life change you for the worse. The best boss I ever had is also one of the nicest people I know. He was the best boss because of his personality, demeanor, and calmness in the midst of major challenges. He worked hard all his life to get to his position. He was an acute, sharp businessman and an effective leader. He had rightfully earned my and many others' respect and trust. I make the effort to keep in contact with him with no other purpose than to stay in touch. With many other previous bosses, the relationship ended when the boss–subordinate relationship came to an end.

Earn Respect as a Leader

Life isn't about getting the better of someone else. Being competitive doesn't require hating your competitor. There is no need to be nasty or demeaning to your subordinates to bring out the best in them or to get their maximum effort. A coach who can quietly plant the desire to win and move his players' hearts will be far more effective than one who makes threats and instills fear. We should strive to be soft in dealing with people, learn to stand absolutely firm on a few core principles, and be decisive in making key life-altering choices.

Being strict and stern doesn't make you a good leader. It doesn't make you a good spouse or parent either. Don't let anyone fool you into believing otherwise. A sincere and caring smile doesn't imply weakness. Outspokenness doesn't mean the person is good at what she does. Loudness shouldn't be mistaken for leadership. Kissing up to superiors and demeaning subordinates are to be avoided. You won't look good by making someone else look bad. Succeeding in your life does not require ruining someone else's. Nastiness is not a requisite to be a great leader.

A great leader can inspire, motivate, and move the hearts of people without raising her voice. I know this to be true—I have seen it in action firsthand and have gotten to practice it while turning around a factory in Clearwater, Florida. People will follow and support a leader whom they respect and trust. And respect and trust must be earned in how you deal with people—those above you, those at your level, and those below you. They don't come automatically with an arbitrary title someone else gives you. The "Silicone IOL" team I had at Clearwater was made up of wonderful people, and they did a fantastic job of turning the entire operation around. In a mere nine months, they achieved improvements way beyond what anyone else in the company thought were possible. Along the way, they taught me a valuable lesson in life and leadership, one I will always cherish.

Having and achieving high aspirations are indeed good things—but the end does not justify the means. Don't let anyone tell you otherwise. Some people create a hard shell to hide behind because that's what they see others do. They think it is what they need to do to survive in the dark ocean, to swim with the sharks. You don't have to be a shark to swim with them. Along with your physical characteristics, you were given a natural personality. God started you off with a great, positive personality. You were meant to be a nice person. Don't let the world influence and change you negatively. You can outswim the sharks without conforming to their ways.

Acknowledge Others

Delegation doesn't mean you only need to acknowledge or associate with your direct reports. Learn people's names—especially of those who may not expect you to know their names. They will be pleasantly surprised. Associate and talk to people. Acknowledge people as you pass them. Learn their spouse's and children's names. Initiate casual conversation. Ask others about their hobbies. Ask how they spent the weekend. Get to know people at an emotional and personal level. This is fundamental to true success and finding meaning in life. Whoever said business is not personal was grossly mistaken. Don't worry so much about the ranks or who may be observing. Be genuine in your interest—people will spot and despise a phony.

> *The path to greatness is along with the others.*
> —*Baltasar Gracian, Spanish priest*

Do Unto Others

If you happen to be in the corporate world, it's much easier to climb the ladder when others are willingly and gladly pushing you up and supporting you. If you get there by stepping on and crushing others, you will lose your footing sooner or later. Falling from the ladder can be an excruciating and humbling experience. Worst of all, people you stepped on previously will have no sympathy for you. In fact, they will be celebrating your well-deserved and long-awaited fall behind your back. I have seen this more times than I care to admit.

Decide how you want to be remembered by your loved ones when you are no longer around. Deal with people fairly, regardless of rank. Treat everyone with respect and dignity. We are all equal in our Creator's eyes. If you trace back far enough, we all came from the same parents. We just happen to play different roles in life.

Do not protect yourself by a fence, but rather by your friends.
—Czech proverb

Life is not a game of predator and prey. It's not about getting the better of someone else. Your life success doesn't require ruining someone else's. You can choose how you deal with others. Keep in mind how you want to be remembered. Do you want to be remembered as a demanding slave driver who always met deadlines no matter what it took? Or would you want to be remembered as an inspiring leader who always brought out the best in people? We all have that choice. People will gladly give their extra effort if you can inspire and touch their hearts. Decide what legacy you want to leave and live accordingly. Treat people fairly, with respect and dignity.

CHAPTER 12
RECOGNIZE TALENT

Just as each of us has one body with many members, and these members do not all have the same function . . . we have different gifts, according to the grace given us.
—Romans 12:4 and 6a

As a child, Aesop's fables were some of my favorite books. Most of us are familiar with "The Tortoise and the Hare." Do you think that was a fair race between these two animals? Was it fair to have a turtle race a rabbit on a hill? Had it been a swimming contest, the tortoise would have won easily over the hare. I realize Aesop's intended lesson is about perseverance, and the tortoise eventually wins through hard work, but I would like to use this story to make another point.

A rabbit's quickness and hopping abilities shouldn't be compared with those of a turtle. A turtle has its own set of strengths and expertise—hopping just isn't one of them. Likewise, a rabbit's value shouldn't be measured by its strength or swimming abilities, or lack thereof. Learn to recognize people's capabilities properly. As you gain more experience and move up within your professional field, the ability to recognize others' talents will become crucial for your success and that of your organization.

Fish Out of Water

Michael Jordan and Tiger Woods would be out of their element on a baseball field. In the case of the former, it was painful, as a devoted fan, to watch him leave the sport he dominated only to struggle miserably in another. The greatest cyclist of all time, Lance Armstrong, would feel out of place in a boxing ring. Mohammed Ali never competed at Wimbledon. Roger Federer wouldn't look so dominant and graceful on the ice rink. Imagining these icons out of their element brings a smile to my face, but this doesn't mean they aren't great athletes. We need to measure their abilities and true greatness by *their* sport. This is an important point to ponder if you are a coach or are in a management position. For the organization to succeed, the players must first be playing the right positions. Waste of talent hurts the individual as well as the organization as a whole.

In the past twenty years of corporate life, especially while working as a consultant, I have witnessed much wasted talent. I wonder how much better we would be as a global society if everyone on this earth found and maximized his or her God-given talent.

I had a friend in college who majored in accounting. She had absolutely no interest in accounting. She selected her major to satisfy her parents' expectations and wishes. Even after the first few basic courses, the fundamental concepts of accounting were difficult for her to grasp. She struggled to graduate in five years even though she took several summer courses. After her gradu-

Pleasure in the job puts perfection in the work.
—Aristotle, ancient Greek philosopher

ation, she was fortunate to get a job offer at one of the bigger and more reputable accounting firms. Sadly, she was absolutely miserable there, and she left the company after only a year. She realized she didn't like numbers and had pursued accounting only to please her parents. She ended up retraining for and doing something completely different. It took her five years of feeling lost in college, the short stint at her first job, and two years of retraining to finally find her talent. After eight years, she finally found happiness at work.

If you lead a group of people, intentionally seek out individuals with different strengths to build your team. A basketball team full of great point guards won't win too many games. A baseball team composed solely of great pitchers won't score enough runs. A relay swim team made up of the world's best backstroke specialists won't be able to outswim the competition. In the same way, an organization full of people who are clones of you—in thought, personality, and especially in expertise and talent—won't succeed. It is more comfortable to surround yourself with people similar to you. Resist this temptation in order to succeed.

Have you chosen the proper career path? Are you maximizing your full potential?

Make the Necessary Changes

Similar to our personal lives, an organization will face its own set of problems, threats, issues (external and internal), setbacks, and many other shark species. These sharks will distract and derail your organization. To triumph over them, you need to have the right people with the right talents in your organization playing the right positions. When you spot a person who is wrong for a given role or position, don't hesitate to make the necessary changes. If uncorrected, it will continue to hurt the individual as well as the organization. Identifying the right talents for yourself and in others is vital to outswimming your sharks as a group. This is how you thrive and win against your competition.

Everyone has his/her own set of talents. If you are a leader of a group, it is your responsibility to identify them and find the proper position for the person. It is possible that a given person's talents will be best maximized at another organization. As the leader, you need to initiate this talk. Do it gently, professionally, and respectfully. You owe it to the person and to the organization.

Each of us is given a talent. Find yours. It will make your work seem much less like, well, work. Whatever it is, develop it. Work hard and continuously to perfect it. Use your talent to enrich the lives of yourself and your loved ones. Recognize and value others' talents. People like and need sincere praise and proper recognition. Help others find and develop their talents if you see them lost and struggling. Wasted talent often equates to wasted life. Help your loved ones to identify and find meaning and fulfillment in their lives.

CHAPTER 13

BE CONFIDENT

They can conquer who believe they can.

—Virgil, ancient Roman poet, best known for the Eclogues,

the Georgics, *and the* Aeneid

After only three months, Reverend Engle dismissed Thomas Edison from school, believing he would never amount to anything. I sometimes wonder what kind of heartless person, a reverend no less, would expel a little kid from school after only a few months. There should be a law against such cruelty. In any case, we all know how the story ends. Edison became one of the most prolific inventors in history, with more than a thousand U.S. patents to his name, as well as many patents in the United Kingdom, France, and Germany. Edison's inventions changed the world.

After his expulsion, Edison's mother homeschooled him and planted the seed of confidence in the heart of her little lad. According to the book *Edison* by Matthew Josephson, Edison recalled later, "My mother was the making of me. She was so true, so sure of me; and I felt I had something to live for, someone I must not disappoint."

When Alexander Graham Bell invented the telephone in 1876, it wasn't exactly a big hit with his first audience. After making a demonstration call, President Rutherford Hayes asked, "That's an amazing invention, but who would ever want to use one of them?"

In the late 1930s, Herbert Mayes, editor of the *Pictorial Review*, commented, "A period movie! About the Civil War! Who needs the Civil War now—who cares?" This was his reaction in rejecting the idea for making the film *Gone with the Wind* based on Margaret Mitchell's 1936 novel. It went on to break just about all box office records of its time.

In 1939, the *New York Times* boldly and confidently declared, "The problem with television is that the people must sit and keep their eyes glued to a screen: the average American family hasn't time for it."

In the early 1940s, a young inventor named Chester Carlson took his idea to twenty corporations, including some of the biggest in the country. They all turned him down. In 1947, after more than five long years of rejections, he finally got a tiny company in Rochester, New York, interested enough to purchase the rights to his invention. His idea involved an electrostatic paper-copying process. The company became the Xerox Corporation we know today.

In 1944, the director of the Blue Book Modeling Agency con-cluded that modeling hopeful Norma Jean Baker was not pho-togenic enough, and there was absolutely no future for her as a model. He told her, "You'd better learn secretarial work." She went on to become Marilyn Monroe.

On September 25th, 1954, the manager of the Grand Ole Opry fired Elvis Presley after one performance and told him, "You ain't goin' nowhere, son. You ought to go back to drivin' a truck."

In 1962, four nervous young men played their first record audition for the executives of the Decca Recording Company. The executives were not impressed. While promptly turning down this group of musi-cians, one of the execu-tives claimed, "We don't like their sound. Groups of guitars are on the way out." The group was called The Beatles.

Success comes from within, not from external forces.
—Ralph Waldo Emerson, American essayist, philosopher, and poet

On August 2nd, 1968, *Business Week* authoritatively and con-vincingly forecasted, "With over fifty foreign cars already on sale here, the Japanese auto industry isn't likely to carve out a big slice of the U.S. market."

The movie *Rocky* won three Oscars in 1976 (Best Picture, Best Director, and Best Film Editing). Until this movie, Sylvester Stallone was hardly the famous actor, screenwriter, and movie producer we know today. The inspiration for *Rocky* came to Stallone after watching a gutsy no-name boxer go the entire distance with the almighty Mohammed Ali. Watching this match sparked an idea and a dream in Stallone. In less than a week, he produced the screenplay for *Rocky* and submitted it to a movie studio via his agent. To Stallone's surprise, the studio offered him $20,000 with either Ryan O'Neal or Burt Reynolds, two prominent actors at the time, playing the main character. Stallone, however, envisioned himself playing the leading role. Despite being broke and desperately needing money, he audaciously turned down the offer. The studio came back with another offer of $80,000, once again with the condition that Stallone give up his dream of playing the lead character. Still, Stallone refused. Other offers soon followed, ultimately reaching $330,000 with Robert Redford possibly playing the role. (Remember, these are mid-1970s dollars, so this is equivalent to well over one million in today's dollars. That's a lot of money, especially for someone struggling to feed himself and pay his rent.) Stallone turned them all down again and again, later admitting that the money was tempting, but he didn't want to live the rest of his life wondering "what if." He chose to believe in himself. To him, his dream was worth more than any amount of money the studio was willing to offer him to stop pursuing it. In order to play the now famed Rocky character himself, Stallone gladly settled for $20,000 for the script and the bare minimum actor's pay of $340 per week. Well, we all know how things turned out. The *Rocky* movies remain one of the most successful series of all time and have since grossed over a billion dollars.

Ken Olson, founder of Digital Equipment Corporation, predicted in 1977, "There is no reason for any individual to have a computer in their home." As a point of comparison, Bill Gates, in his twenties, had a vision of placing a personal computer in everyone's home. This is a vision no one shared at the time, except for a handful of people. Realization of his dream made Gates the wealthiest individual on this planet.

Fred Smith, the founder of FedEx, first presented his idea of an overnight delivery service as a term paper while he was a Yale undergraduate. His professor was less than enthused with the concept. He did not think the radical idea was feasible. This is the comment Fred Smith received from his Yale management professor: "The concept is interesting and well-formed, but in order to earn better than a C, the idea must be feasible." The professor, with all his experience and expertise, found the hub and spoke concept to be impractical. There were additional obstacles to overcome when Smith actually tried to launch his company several years later. Given the complex government regulations around inter-state transportation at the time (1970s), it was a difficult task to sell the unproven idea to venture capitalists and Wall Street. Multiple market researchers concluded that the business model would utterly fail (fortunately, the results of these studies came out after the financing was completed). Smith believed in his own idea and abilities and chose to ignore the naysayers. Today, FedEx's annual revenue is approximately $40 billion, and it employs over 220,000 people globally. FedEx defined fast and reliable delivery and is one of the greatest entrepreneurial success stories.

After a near-fatal car accident in 1949, Ben Hogan, a professional golfer, was told by his doctors that he would never walk again. Despite resulting lifelong circulation problems and other physical limitations from a double-fracture of the pelvis, a fractured collarbone, a left ankle fracture, a chipped rib, and near-fatal blood clots, Ben Hogan not only walked again, he continued to win championships. His greatest year came four years after the accident, in the 1953 season, when he won five of the six tournaments he entered and the first three major championships of the year (a feat now dubbed "the Hogan Slam"). It still stands among the greatest single seasons in the history of professional golf.

Wilma Rudolph was the twentieth of twenty-two children. She was born prematurely and her survival was doubtful from the very beginning. When she was four years old, she contracted double pneumonia and scarlet fever, which left her with a paralyzed left leg. It took nine years before she could remove the metal leg brace and begin to walk, albeit slowly and awkwardly, on her own. As soon as she could walk, however, she decided to fulfill her dream of becoming a runner. She entered a race and came in last. For the next few years, she came in last in every race she entered. Everyone told her to quit, but she was persistent and kept to her rigorous training. Several years later, she actually won a race. And then another win followed. She eventually started winning every race she entered and transformed herself into the fastest woman in the world. The little girl, who was once told she would never walk again by medical experts, ultimately went on to win three gold medals at the 1960 Rome Olympic Games.

Park Ji Sung, a fellow native of South Korea, is a favorite soccer player of mine. Throughout his life, he was often dismissed due to his small physical frame. Despite his incredible work ethic and discipline, he barely made it to a small college team and eventually as a pro with a second-tier Japanese league. He eventually led his team to the first Emperor's Cup in its history. Park ignored the naysayers who said he wasn't big enough and devoted himself to achieving his dream. In 2002, Park was selected for South Korea's World Cup Team and played every game in my home country's extraordinary and exciting run to the semifinals. Watching him outmaneuver much bigger players during the Cup was simply awe-inspiring. Park became an instant national hero when he scored the winning goal in a critical game against Portugal. Through self-confidence, determination, and hard work, Park had finally silenced all his critics and turned the entire nation of forty-five million people into his devoted fans. He now plays for Manchester United, in the ultracompetitive, physically grueling English Premier League. To date, he remains the only Asian to be part of the Champions League semifinals three different times.

Achieve Your Own Success

The examples could go on and on. The point I want to make is that you can create a similar heartwarming, triumphant story with your own life. Believe in yourself and devote yourself to achieving your own success. Do not rely on others to come and rescue you. Ignore all naysayers, especially in times of doubt and uncertainty. Don't let them or any other sharks in your life derail you. Take control of your own life and destiny.

Everyone has at least one naysayer in his or her life. I had, and still have, many in my life. Forget these naysayers—don't let them persuade you to stop chasing your dreams and goals. There is no point in arguing with them. The best way to silence your critics is to prove them wrong by succeeding. There is a rumor that years later Fred Smith sent his term paper back to his professor for a reevaluation. I wonder how the professor felt. I wonder how the Grand Ole Opry manager felt when he saw Elvis performing on TV.

Recognize Unintentional Naysayers

Unfortunately, our naysayers may include our loved ones giving us well-intended advice. These loving people, too, can drain confidence and optimism from us. They can be our parents, our spouse, our relatives, or our friends. Learn to swim around these unintentional sharks. Listen carefully to their advice, suggestions, and worries, and thank them sincerely for their concern. Consider it objectively and make the final decision yourself. It is very possible that their point is valid. If that's the case, then you need to modify your goals and actions.

But there are two other, perhaps unconscious, motives for their discouragement. First, they may fear that you will fail. They prefer you to play it safe even if it means compromising your dreams and settling for far less than what you are capable of. Their perceived fear of your failure far outweighs the opportunity and possibility ahead.

The future belongs to those who believe in the beauty of their dreams.
—Eleanor Roosevelt, First Lady of the United States, wife of President Franklin D. Roosevelt

Second, they may fear that if you manage to succeed, you will disrupt the "pack order" in which you belong. Should you become a successful artist, should you be accepted into an Ivy League school, should you become a well-respected lawyer, should you achieve lofty financial goals, you will move up in the arbitrary pack order, disrupt the invisible hierarchy, break the comfortable and well-established status quo, and so on. This potential makes them uncomfortable. They prefer the familiarity and the sense of false security that comes with the status quo. Learn to identify these instances. Remember, when it comes to your own life, you must make the final decision in setting your goals and writing your story. All others are supporting cast members.

What if You Are Your Own Naysayer?

What if you happen to be the biggest critic of your own life? What if you represent one of the biggest sharks in your own life?

Most of us have two sides to ourselves. There is the confident self who believes we can and will achieve all that we set out to do. And then there is the self-doubter in all of us. This side causes us to second-guess ourselves and our abilities, credentials, accomplishments, and potential. When we become our own biggest naysayer, we start questioning whether we are truly deserving of happiness and success in our lives. The naysayer in us tries to convince us that we are not quite good enough. This dark side of us disguises our deepest fears as experience and intelligence. The self-naysayer in us builds a convincing argument for maintaining the status quo, blinding us from seeing the opportunities around us.

Identify and overcome this tendency. Demolish self-perceived limitations. Do not allow yourself to become your own naysayer. Give yourself the credit you deserve. You are often far more capable than you consider yourself.

Caution

There is a difference between self-confidence and arrogance. There is a difference between persistence and stubbornness. There is a difference between patient devotion and plain foolishness. There is a difference between trusting yourself and lacking common sense.

I am reminded of these facts when I watch auditions for *American Idol*, a popular reality TV show in the United States for the past nine or ten years. Each season, thousands, if not tens of thousands, of people line up for an opportunity to showcase their vocal talents. The sad truth is that the vast majority of these people simply are not good singers. In most cases, it's obvious to others, especially the judges, within a few seconds. What's amazing to me is that these people are so self-delusional.

Most people consider persistence and patience to be two noble traits. Indeed, these are qualities we must adopt for ourselves. They are both crucial ingredients in pursuing our dreams and achieving our success. It is equally and extremely important, however, to be able to distinguish these two traits from stubbornness and foolishness.

What are the differences between them? Well, a stubborn person hates to admit being wrong. Stubbornness implies that you intend to continue on a path despite a plethora of evidence that you should not.

Persistence and patience are two essential virtues required to achieve your worthwhile goals. Stubbornness and foolishness will prohibit and actually lead you farther away from your goals. In many cases, stubbornness and foolishness will lead you into setting the wrong goals.

As the Bible prudently warns, "Have sane estimates of your capabilities" (Romans 12:3). Be aware of your strengths. When you teach, do people listen and learn? When you lead, do people willingly follow? If you work as a consultant, do people take your advice seriously? What are you naturally good at? Do you naturally make people laugh? When you sing, do people find it soothing or enjoyable? Are you gifted athletically? We are all given unique talents. Make sure you identify yours. Use them to better yourself and those around you.

Choose to believe in yourself, especially when no one else does. Learn to ignore the naysayers. You have the ultimate control of what you make of your own life. Take full accountability of the decisions you make and their consequences. Work hard to silence your critics. Use them to light your fire. Use them and all other sharks in your life to motivate yourself.

CHAPTER 14

BEWARE THE "HAMMER SYNDROME"

Arrogance diminishes wisdom.

—Arabian proverb

Back in the late 1990s, I worked for a client in the beautiful and picturesque small town of Latrobe, Pennsylvania, approximately thirty miles west of Pittsburgh. It's the home of legendary golfer Arnold Palmer, Mr. Rogers (famous for his "It's a Beautiful Day in the Neighborhood" children's song), and Rolling Rock beer in the original green bottles. In the fall, when the leaves start changing colors, Latrobe becomes one of the most scenic places on earth. The sheer natural beauty of the town and nearby surroundings cannot be justly described in words. Latrobe is also the place where the Pittsburgh Steelers hold their summer camp. They sure know how to pick a great spot!

The project I was on was a big success. We worked closely with the client to rationalize their product offering and to reduce inventory levels. My consulting company received a bonus for meeting certain predetermined stretch objectives. It was a big win for the consulting company I worked for, but more importantly, it was a big win for the customer.

What I found even more rewarding than the results were the relationships I formed. The people were extremely nice and went way above what's required to make someone feel at home. As a result, I very much enjoyed being in Latrobe, so much so that I decided to live there for six months instead of flying back home to Chicago every weekend. When the project ended, the people threw a heartwarming going-away party for me, complete with many gifts, including a six-pack of Rolling Rock beer. It felt like leaving a decade-long job rather than a temporary project.

He who is good with a hammer thinks everything is a nail.
—Anonymous

On one of my last days there, one of the team members gave me this insightful piece of advice, which has stayed with me after more than a decade: "He who is good with a hammer thinks everything is a nail."

The individual who gave me this advice was a good man with extensive and diverse life experiences along with a ton of life stories. We had become friends during my stay in Latrobe. He was more than happy and willing to share his stories with me over casual dinners filled with laughter. The statement was his way of telling me that we had done well together in the project. It was also his subtle way of cautioning me not to let my expertise and strengths become weaknesses in the future. Yes, our strength, when overplayed, can become our biggest weakness and shortfall.

We Often See Only What We Have Been Trained to See

There was a study conducted, I believe at Carnegie Mellon University, back in the 1980s in which a team of experts was brought together to solve a rather complex business case. These experts were world renowned in their respective areas. The meeting must have resembled a gathering of the world's greatest minds. The business case was presented with detailed background along with pages and pages of facts and data to enable proper decision making. The entire team of experts held an extensive and collective discussion. After the grueling group session, each expert was asked to work individually and come back with specific recommendations on how to solve the complex business issue.

Unfortunately, the world-leading experts could not agree on the solution. In fact, the experts could not agree on the fundamental, underlying problems. What was happening? You guessed it—the "hammer syndrome." The accounting expert clearly saw the business facing enormous accounting issues causing detrimental consequences to the business. The HR expert was convinced the root cause was an obvious HR issue. The operations expert had never seen such poor results from production facilities and pointed to urgent operational improvement opportunities. The strategist thoroughly analyzed the competitive environment and argued for a quick and drastic change in the corporate direction before they fell off the cliff. The IT expert acutely pointed out how the horribly outdated systems

The trouble with ignorance is that it picks up confidence as it goes along.
—Arnold Glasow, American humorist

were creating inefficiency and had a clear picture for what new systems were needed and how they should all be integrated.

To succeed in life, you need to excel in your chosen field. But you must be careful not to let your expertise blind you. To outswim the sharks and succeed in life, be aware of this potential pitfall—in yourself and in others. Learn to develop solutions based on the problems. Avoid molding the problems to fit your expertise and/or predefined solutions. As a relatively young consultant just starting to develop my own niche of expertise, this was a valuable lesson and timely advice.

Remove Your Tinted Glasses to Appreciate the True View

Put on a pair of dark sunglasses and everything will appear a little dimmer. If your sunglasses happen to have brown-tinted lenses, everything will seem to have a brown hue. These tinted lenses represent certain biases or predetermined conclusions. With these glasses on, you will only see things that will reinforce your beliefs.

I consider myself an expert on two particular processes and performance improvement tools: Lean and Six Sigma. I have successfully implemented these two philosophies and techniques in numerous situations. But only after twenty years have I come to realize that not everything in life can be completely solved with my limited, niche expertise.

Devote yourself to exceling in your chosen field. At the same time, be open-minded; it's good to recognize your strength, but be aware there may be other sides to the issue at hand. Beware the hammer syndrome. Don't let your confidence overgrow to become a shark in your life.

CHAPTER 15

FOCUS ON BOTH QUANTITY AND QUALITY

Quality is free, but only to those who are willing to pay heavily for it.
—*Philip Crosby, American business philosopher and quality expert*

During my early consulting days, I was out at a dinner in Wichita, Kansas, with several coworkers and clients. As a side comment, Wichita has surprisingly many great restaurants. I got to enjoy most, if not all, of them multiple times during my nine-month stay. If you have a local friend or two who can advise you on where to go, Wichita is a wonderful midwestern city. I still have a friend there whom I have been meaning to visit for awhile. It's been more than a decade since I left Wichita, but I remember his wife used to make the best red hot sauce in the world. Just thinking about it makes my mouth water.

Let me get back to the story. After dinner, as the conversation turned more casual, one of the younger, jovial clients stated, "What I lacked in quality, I certainly tried my best to make up in quantity." He was referring to his string of short-term girlfriends and other promiscuous relationships he had had back in college. He said it jokingly of course, and we all had a good chuckle.

Several years later, in a much more serious manner and setting, I was given well-intended advice by a mentor, who remains today one of my lifelong friends: "When you must, choose quality over quantity." It sounded a bit trite at the time, and after adding another decade of life experiences of my own, I came to disagree with this particular advice.

The notion that quality is more important than quantity has early roots and is backed by several notable figures. Nearly two thousand years ago, one of the better-known Roman philosophers of the time, Lucius Annaeus Seneca, stated, "It is quality rather than quantity that matters." By the way, Seneca was one of the main counselors to Nero, the emperor best known for his tyranny and extravagance, and regarded as the emperor who "fiddled while Rome burned." Taking this into account, one can argue whether Seneca's suggestions should be taken seriously. Almost a century ago, Mahatma Gandhi also made a case for quality over quantity when he advised, "It is the quality of our work which will please god and not the quantity."

It may be that I have yet to face a dire situation that required me to pick one or the other. But my own experiences and observations to date tell me this is not the proper approach to life. Quantity should not be substituted for quality, and quality should not be substituted for quantity. In most instances, I personally found the quality vs. quantity debate to be irrelevant. This is especially the case when it comes to building and maintaining personal relationships.

It is a funny thing about life: if you refuse to accept anything but the best you very often get it.
—W. Somerset Maugham, French-born English novelist, playwright, and short-story writer

Our bodies need a balanced diet of protein, carbohydrates, and fat for proper nutrition; if one is substituted for another, there will certainly be adverse health consequences in the long term. Likewise, both quantity and quality are equally important. One should not be substituted for another. Careful balance must be maintained for a healthy life and relationships with others.

An automobile needs four wheels to balance and function properly. All of them are equally important. A bigger front right tire cannot offset a smaller rear left tire. The choice of quality over quantity, or vice versa, makes very little sense in real life.

Now, let's consider specific life challenges that most of us can relate to.

Are you spending enough time with your loved ones? Are you too busy to spend sufficient time with your spouse and children? Or do you find yourself trying to make up for a lack of quantity with quality? Unfortunately, it cannot be done. Quantity cannot be substituted with quality. Your loved ones need your time. "Quality" time alone is not sufficient if you are not sharing enough of it. Those who spend a lot of time with their children are more likely to have more quality moments with them. These quality moments often happen spontaneously. They cannot be planned, scheduled, or produced. Quality and quantity often come together.

If you are spending enough time with your family, are you spending it meaningfully? Are you taking each other for granted? Are you actively listening to your children? Or is your time together merely physically being in the same house at the same time? Is everyone in the same house but in separate rooms doing different things? Quantity of time does not make up for poor quality.

If you are an athlete or at least interested in staying in shape, it is the frequency and duration of your training sessions (quantity) combined with the intensity of your workouts (quality) that matter. If you only visit the gym once a week, it's simply not enough to get into top shape. Similarly, even if you are able to go on a daily basis, if your sessions aren't strenuous enough, you are just wasting your time. Quantity and quality are equally important.

QUALITY IS MADE POSSIBLE ONLY BY QUANTITY

During my research for this book, I found the following relevant story on a blog by Benjamin Sternke that is worth sharing.

QUALITY VS. QUANTITY

The ceramics teacher announced on opening day that he was dividing the class into two groups. All those on the left side of the studio, he said, would be graded solely on the quantity of work they produced; all those on the right solely on its quality. His procedure was simple: on the final day of class he would bring in his bathroom scales and weigh the work of the "quantity" group: fifty pounds of pots rated an "A," forty pounds a "B," and so on. Those being graded on "quality," however, needed to produce only one pot—albeit a perfect one—to get an "A." Well, came grading time and a curious fact emerged: the works of highest quality were all produced by the group being graded for quantity. It seems that while the "quantity" group was busily churning out piles of work—and learning from their mistakes—the "quality" group had sat theorizing about perfection, and in the end had little more to show for their efforts than grandiose theories and a pile of dead clay.

This story serves as a reminder that quality and quantity often come together. In this particular case, quantity produced quality. You need to practice a lot to become good at your chosen field. Don't compromise one for the other. They are equally important—find the right balance. This story also reiterates another point made earlier in this book: the importance of taking action toward your goals. Our time in this world is limited. Resist the temptation to stand still. Avoid the analysis-till-paralysis syndrome. Make the effort to reach your full potential. Albeit essential, defining your life goals is only the first step. It alone is not sufficient. Work diligently to realize your life goals.

I have a close friend named Stuart who lives in London. He is an avid distance runner. He has already run multiple ultramarathons, and he continues to practice and plans to travel the world to compete in future events. While he and his wonderful girlfriend Susie were visiting me in Seoul in 2009, he described his most recent experience of running a marathon per day for six consecutive days and then running the equivalent of two marathons on the last day. A marathon is 26 miles long (42 kilometers). As if this isn't difficult enough, the entire event took place in the desert under the scorching and unforgiving sun and in the midst of excruciating heat. Moreover, all competitors were required to carry backpacks containing everyday necessities while running. Indeed, this particular sport is the ultimate test of human determination and extreme physical exhaustion. To properly prepare himself, Stuart runs a lot (quantity) and with great intensity (quality). To compete at this borderline crazy sport, you simply cannot substitute quantity with quality and vice versa. Both are equally and extremely important. The whole issue of quantity vs. quality has no relevance in this case and many others. They often come together and are inseparable.

Consistently writing many mediocre reports won't get you far at work. Having had one great year of performance in the past but not being able to repeat it will make you a has-been. I have known and worked with both of these types during the past twenty years. They were excluded from the high-potential list and were not seriously considered when it came time for promotions. If we want to excel at work and climb the corporate ladder, we need great performance year after year. Past accomplishments, regardless of how great, do not guarantee a bright future. We need to produce both quantity and quality. We need to work harder than our peers to get ahead. We need to do this in the midst of whatever sharks we have in our lives. Yes, it isn't easy to swim with and outswim the sharks. But be assured, it can be done.

For a sports franchise, years of average seasons will trap it in a state of complacency and the attendance will drop. A championship won a decade ago will cause fans to reminisce about the good old days, hoping for the return to glory in the future, if it ever comes. In either case, there is no excitement in the present. There is no excitement in being average or dwelling in the past. To strive for greatness, one needs to repeat championship-level performance consistently.

If you are in the entertainment industry, having many average songs or being in many average movies will only make you average. If you had one hit but can't repeat it, people will consider you a one-hit wonder and will soon forget you.

The right balance of quantity and quality are needed to succeed in life—in your relationships with your loved ones as well as in your chosen professional field.

How many friends do you have? How many close people do you have in your life? Would you like to have one hundred acquaintances, ones whom you enjoy being with but who are not necessarily close enough to share your deepest thoughts and to rely on when times are tough? Or would you like to associate mainly with only one person throughout your entire life? Perhaps the latter sounds more noble, but I believe the practical and ideal answer lies somewhere in between the two extremes.

Life is all about relationships, enjoying each others' company and enriching each others' lives. You need the proper mix of quality and quantity. I have a handful of people in my life who mean the world to me. They are the highest priorities in my life. Just like many other important things in life, it takes time and conscious effort to maintain our relationships, and through time our relationships and friendships have deepened and matured. The ample quantity of time spent together boosts the quality of our relationship, and the quality of time when we are together makes me want to spend more time with them. Quality and quantity are complementary when it comes to my personal relationships.

Quantity should not be compromised for the sake of quality. Similarly, quality makes a poor substitute for quantity. Spend enough time with your loved ones and doing what's important to you. And make sure the time you spend is of high quality. Just as all four tires on your car are equally important and one cannot make up for another, quantity and quality also cannot be separated or one compromised for the other.

CHAPTER 16

OVERCOME OBSTACLES AND CHALLENGES

Obstacles are those frightful things you see when you take your eyes off your goal.
—*Henry Ford, founder of Ford Motor Company*

Just in case you are unfamiliar with the story of Job in the Old Testament, here is a synopsis. Job was a good man living in the land of Uz. He is described as "blameless and upright." He was by far the wealthiest man in town, possessing a great number of sheep, camels, oxen, and donkeys. Evidently, this is how one's net worth in the Old Testament days was measured in absence of stocks and fancy new cars. Job was also blessed with seven sons and three daughters. They apparently enjoyed each other's company and got along very well, often throwing parties and inviting each other. Simply put, Job had a wonderful life. He had no financial worries and a happy family.

Then one day it all came down in a series of tragic events. The house collapsed during one of the regular gatherings, killing all of his ten children. All his possessions were stolen or destroyed in a fire. Only a few servants remained to inform Job of the disaster and misfortune.

Job was a man who had it all. And he lost it all in the blink of an eye. I wonder what must have gone through his head on that dreadful, tragic day. He did not deserve what happened, and he certainly had no control over the events. His reaction, something he had total control of, is worth noting. The Bible states, "In all this, Job did not sin by charging God with wrongdoing" (Job 1:22). God does not reward Job for his noble attitude and integrity, at least not initially. In fact, He does the opposite—the good Lord allows the devil to afflict Job with "painful sores from the soles of his feet to the top of his head" (Job 2:7). In frustration, his wife, the only surviving family member, turns against him: "Are you still holding on to your integrity? Curse God and die!" (Job 2:9). His three closest friends come with the right intention to comfort, but instead they end up making various self-righteous accusations and claims against Job. Talk about kicking someone when they are down.

I can't fathom how Job must have felt. Sudden loss of your own sons and daughters. Dealing with the death of your faithful servants. Going from having it all to nothing at all in an instant. Torment from painful sores covering your entire body. Wife turning against you. Friends making accusations. To a much lesser degree, I think we can all relate to Job's loneliness and state of frustration.

Amazingly, Job maintained his composure and sanity. As a result, here's how his story ends: "The Lord blessed the latter part of Job's life more than the first. He had fourteen thousand sheep, six thousand camels, a thousand yoke of oxen, and a thousand donkeys. And he also had seven sons and three daughters" (Job 42:12 and 13).

We could never learn to be brave and patient if there were only joy in the world.

—Helen Keller, American author, political activist, and lecturer who prevailed over her blindness and deafness

Job chose to deal with the unexpected turn of events with integrity and maintained his composure. We can all make a similar choice when we are faced with our own adversity.

In just about all walks of life, there are examples of overcoming unexpected tragedies and adverse events. In each case, it took unwavering focus and dedication to overcome these obstacles. These are the most unlikely comeback stories. These individuals, when confronted with what appeared to be a ferocious shark attack in their lives, faced the challenge head-on and triumphed. These stories inspire us. They give us hope that we, too, can face and outswim any shark species thrown into our lives.

And we can. It won't be easy, but the choice is ours. We can go on and on with real-life comeback stories, but here are a few short examples.

Lance Armstrong

Lance Armstrong was diagnosed with testicular cancer in 1996. The doctors gave him less than a one percent chance of living. Even if he were to miraculously survive, virtually no one expected him to return to his profession and compete in one of the most grueling sports. Armstrong dealt with his adversity head-on and fought back. Not only did he survive, he returned to cycling and won the Tour de France in 1999, his first of what would be seven consecutive yellow jerseys. In the process, he motivated and won the admiration of millions of people around the world. He has also popularized cycling both as a spectator sport and as a hobby in many countries. His total dominance in his chosen field ended only upon his initial retirement in 2005. Four years later, Armstrong came out of retirement and had a podium finish in 2009. It's a pretty impressive comeback for someone the medical experts gave less than a one percent chance of living.

Harley-Davidson

On the verge of bankruptcy in the early 1980s, Harley-Davidson found itself facing severe market conditions and heavy foreign competition from Honda, Suzuki, Kawasaki, and Yamaha. The once legendary motorcycle manufacturer's annual loss mounted to $16 million, and its market share had dwindled to 15 percent. No one expected the once mighty Harley-Davidson brand to survive.

Clyde Fessler, then CEO of Harley-Davidson, and his team were determined to turn their last remaining American motorcycle manufacturer from the rust belt of the Midwest into a Fortune 500 company success story. They did it by not only focusing on the four fundamental Ps of marketing (product, price, place, and promotion), but also by adding a fifth P—people, the most important ingredient in any business turnaround.

To make operational improvements, they sent their manufacturing and engineering personnel to Japan to study how the Japanese made motorcycles. (It was called "industrial spying" back then; today it's more commonly referred to as "benchmarking.") What they came back with compelled Harley-Davidson to introduce just-in-time inventory, statistical process control, employee involvement, and new manufacturing processes. Going against the grain, the styling department implemented a classical, evolutionary design for motorcycles, rather than the revolutionary design of something new every year from the competition. To focus on the *people* factor, they created HOG (Harley Owners Group) to create a sense of community and an emotional lifestyle experience as well as to bond with customers. HOG now has close to half a million members throughout the world and has raised over $25 million for the Muscular Dystrophy Association. A few former colleagues of mine are HOG members, and if they are any indication, HOG is a group of devoted and enthusiastic fans.

As a result of the turnaround, Harley-Davidson made an annual profit of $1.6 billion and its market share recovered to 49 percent by the mid-1990s. The company has been held up as one of the great business turnaround stories of all time.

Nicolo Paganini

Gifted nineteenth-century violinist Nicolo Paganini's most memorable concert and greatest professional moment occurred in Italy while he was performing with a full orchestra before a packed house. As usual, his technique was incredible, his tone was fantastic, and his audience dearly loved him. Toward the end of the concert, one string on his violin snapped. Paganini simply shook his head and continued to play, improvising beautifully with the remaining three strings.

Then to everyone's surprise, a second string broke. And shortly thereafter, a third. Almost like a slapstick comedy, Paganini stood there with three strings dangling from his Stradivarius. The vast majority of people would have stopped the performance momentarily and changed to another violin. Instead, Paganini stood his ground and calmly completed the difficult number on the one remaining string. Such reactions separate greatness from the average. You can guess the audience's reaction and the appreciation.

Expect Bumps Along the Way

There will undoubtedly be bumps in life. One of your loved ones may succumb to illness. You may lose your job with no advance notice. You may suffer a significant financial and/or emotional loss. You will one day be disappointed with your performance at an athletic event, concert hall, speaking engagement, whatever. These things will happen, and you will have very little control over them. But you can make the decision to bounce back. Get up and dust off. Stay on track of your long-term goals. You can let life have the better of you, or you can stand up and try again.

Life will throw you curveballs. There will be shark attacks in everyone's lives. How one chooses to deal with them will separate the winners from the rest.

Most people will succumb to them and reflect on what could have been. You can choose to face and overcome your adversity—whatever it may be. Stand up to your obstacles and do something about them. You will find that they haven't half the strength you think they have. Prove to others and more importantly to yourself that you are bigger than whatever problem has been thrown at you. Use adversity and tragedy as stepping-stones to become stronger as an organization and/or as a person.

Deal wisely with the obstacles and challenges. There will certainly be many shark attacks along the way. Stay on track and maintain your composure. Whatever obstacle you may be facing at this moment, think of it as an opportunity to create your own comeback story. Remember, you are bigger than any of the shark species allowed in your life. Overcome obstacles and challenges.

CHAPTER 17

WILL MOMMY LOVE ME HALF AS MUCH? LEARN TO SHARE

A candle loses nothing by lighting another candle.
—Father James Keller, Roman Catholic priest and founder of
The Christophers, a Christian inspirational group

I was once engaged to a wonderful woman named Jill. Although things did not work out between us, we remain good friends. For this, I am truly grateful. And it is true that God knows us better than we know ourselves. It took several years for me to get over the breakup, but I have since met and eventually married the most amazing and precious woman in the world.

While we were dating, I had the pleasant opportunities to meet all of Jill's immediate family members, including a little boy named Hugh. Huey, as he was often called, was one of Jill's many nephews. He must be around eleven or twelve years old by now, and I am sure he has gotten much taller and bigger since I saw him last. But in my mind, I still cherish the image of little Huey as a perpetual four-year-old. He was an absolutely adorable kid with a big round face, two enormous, sparkling eyes, and a contagious ear-to-ear smile, and he was terrified of fireworks.

While visiting Jill's family in Indianapolis, I remember one particular occasion when Huey came to me with a serious look on his face—not the expression you would expect from a four-year-old who should be living a carefree life. With tear-swelled eyes, which made them look even bigger and brighter, Huey asked, "Uncle Joong, will mommy love me half as much?" You see, his mother was eight months pregnant at the time.

Little Huey's math was wrong, as he already had a just-as-adorable older sister named Alex and a younger baby brother named Isaac. Little Isaac, by the way, was going through the terrible twos and causing all kinds of havoc around the house. They were the cutest set of siblings, born to the two most patient and perfect Catholic parents. These children were extremely fortunate to have each other and to be raised in such a loving family.

Little Huey's impending sibling would be the fourth child in the family. With him being so young, I first had to restrain myself from correcting his math. I then had to stop myself from bursting into laughter. Instead, I tried to assure him that he had nothing to worry about, that his mother would love him just the same, if not more. I reminded him that his mommy's love didn't lessen with more kids in the house. He seemed pretty satisfied and assured with the answer, which by the way made me think I may one day make a good father.

Shared grief is half the sorrow, but happiness when shared, is doubled.

—Anonymous

I wonder how many of us adults act like the four-year-old Huey. When it comes to the most precious things in life, such as love, laughter, joy, knowledge, and experience, sharing does not mean reducing your portion.

Don't Be an Information Hoarder

At work there are many whom I call information hoarders. These are the people who don't like to share what they know. For them, information is power. It's what gives them an edge over others. They feel self-important with the closely held information and create an illusion of being in an inner circle of some sort. Taken to an extreme, they become paranoid; if they shared what they knew, the company would "love" them only half as much and their value would immediately dwindle.

Perhaps these habits were formed to preserve job security. Or perhaps these habits were learned out of survival instinct after being burned in the past. Regardless of how they were formed, it is crucial to recognize and correct this detrimental habit for personal and organizational success. If these people move up within the organization uncorrected, functional silos are the eventual and inevitable consequence. Sadly, I have seen far too many cases of this behavior in real life.

Don't Be a Stop Sign

Managers and others in authority can play a similar game. They get false self-fulfillment out of having to approve anything and everything. They insist on having to review, authorize, and approve everything their direct and indirect subordinates do. For them, proper delegation equates to lessened importance. They love creating and being a part of unnecessary committees— not to do the actual work, but to play the judge. The office comes to a halt when they are away. They constantly complain about this, but in actuality, it makes them feel important and valued. "The office will never survive without me being there," they tell themselves. This is all a self-created mirage and is destructive to personal and organizational success. These traits represent typical behaviors of human sharks.

One of the best ways to lead people is to inspire them—to create a strong desire in people's hearts to do what's best for the organization as a whole. Acting like a stop sign isn't leadership. This is how you become a shark in other people's lives and in your organization. You may have the right intentions, but it is important to recognize and correct these shark-like behaviors, if they exist.

Stop acting like a four-year-old and share what you have. Share information and knowledge. This does not mean you should share company secrets with competitors; we are talking about sharing with the people you know you should share with. Include the right people in making decisions. Don't make decisions based on office politics, which is often the biggest shark that prohibits an organization from reaching its true potential. Involve everyone who should be in the loop. Don't intentionally leave out a peer who has expressed an opposing opinion. Before you send an important e-mail, double-check your distribution list to make sure you have included all relevant individuals. When it comes to communication and sharing, it is always better to overdo it than the alternative.

New People Bring Value

Hiring another competent person in your organization doesn't reduce your value. A new person is another opportunity for learning, especially if the person is exceptionally talented in his or her chosen area. Think what would happen if a professional sports team restricted anyone young and promising from joining the team.

A mother's love for her child does not diminish with the arrival of another. The beauty and the serenity of a sunset over the calm and peaceful ocean are not reduced when others are present. Learn to share. It's a great way to enhance the lives of others.

Growing Award-Winning Produce

In his book *How to Talk Well*, James Bender tells a story of an award-winning corn farmer. Each year this farmer entered his corn in the state fair, and he won the blue ribbon multiple times. One year a newspaper reporter, wanting to discover the secret behind his success, is surprised to learn that this farmer freely shares his award-winning corn seeds with his neighbors. The reporter is curious as to why anyone would share his best corn seeds with his competitors. In response, the farmer replies:

> Didn't you know? The wind picks up pollen from the ripening corn and swirls it from field to field. If my neighbors grow inferior corn, cross-pollination will steadily degrade the quality of my corn. If I am to grow good corn, I must help my neighbors grow good corn.

The farmer understood the beauty and wonders behind sharing. He knew he could enrich himself only by enriching others around him. Learn to share. Pass along your knowledge. Let others gain from your experience. Use your life to improve the lives of others.

Share your know-how. If you are a technician, share the technique. If you are an athlete, share your successful workout regimen with your teammates. This will help you win as a team. Share your effective diet secrets with your coworkers. This won't cause you to gain your weight back. In fact, you can encourage each other on your way to thinner, healthier bodies. Share the knowledge. Share the results and details of your analysis. Share your life experiences with those who will benefit from hearing about them. This is how you become better as an individual and as a group.

PART IV

OUTSWIMMING THE SHARKS

CHAPTER 18

YOU DON'T HAVE TO BE A SHARK TO SWIM WITH AND OUTSWIM THEM

Do not conform any longer to the pattern of this world.

—*Romans 12:2a*

The human version of sharks can sometimes take the form of extremely career-driven people who will stop at nothing to attain their goals. Regardless of one's chosen career path, everyone has at least one of these shark species in his or her life. You can swim with and outswim your sharks without succumbing or resorting to their nefarious ways.

There is no problem whatsoever with having lofty goals. It's the shark's approach you must never emulate or be contaminated with. These sharks exemplify how not to behave, how you shouldn't approach and live your life. If necessary, these sharks will compromise their integrity, marriage, friendship, the law, and anything else they feel keeps them from getting what they want. "It's not illegal unless you get caught" is their motto. They are needlessly ferocious, pointlessly aggressive, and on a constant lookout for blood. They fool themselves into believing successes in their own lives require failures in other people's lives. They are constantly lurking in the dark for their next prey to devour. They smell blood from miles away and come together when it's feeding time. They gather to devour the weak. When it's done, they all go their separate ways looking for their next victim. They will cheat, they will lie, they will torture the weak, they will kiss up to gain favor, they will backstab in a heartbeat. They will stop at nothing for their personal gain.

You need to beware. These sharks' overly and needlessly aggressive nature and dishonest ways are contagious. You must learn to stay immune. Don't let them change you for the worse. Despite what you may believe, truly successful people are an entirely different species.

You don't have to adopt the attitude and the lifestyle of a shark to find a meaningful purpose, set worthy goals, and live a successful life. You can make the choice not to be one of them. You can remain firm on your principles and stand tall against your sharks. Swimming with the sharks doesn't require you to be one. You can outswim them all without resorting to their ways. Think of the person you admire the most in life, the person you want to emulate. Would you describe this person as a shark?

Be a Dolphin in the Midst—Adopt These Anti-shark Behaviors

Help people in need. Sharks collectively select and devour the perceived weakest. You don't need to mimic their predatory behavior. Choose to defend the weak, rather than gathering to devour them. This is how you gain trust and respect.

Get to know people as people, not as your subordinates, peers, bosses, suppliers, customers, or competitors. Learn their names, nicknames, spouses' names, background, hobbies, past experiences, childhood dreams, future plans, pet peeves, and passions. This takes time and effort, but there are few more rewarding life experiences than getting to know someone at a deep and personal level.

He who trims himself to suit everyone will soon whittle himself away.
—Raymond Hull, Canadian playwright, television screenwriter, and lecturer

Be positive rather than joining in on cynicism. Negativity is highly contagious. You don't have to be one of the carriers.

Form and stand firm on your own opinions rather than surveying to determine the most popular, politically correct stance. Your opinions should be your opinions. If you don't have an opinion on a particular topic, be honest about it. There is no rule stating you must have an adamant opinion about everything in life.

Work harder if you want to be promoted or chosen. Choose not to leverage any personal connections you may have. The end does not justify the means. It's good to be ambitious, but make sure you go up the ladder in the right way—the honorable way. You will learn that it's easier to move up and stay atop when others push you up and support you.

Be humble and credit others whenever warranted rather than angling accomplishments for your own glory. One of my former colleagues once told me, "There is nothing we can't achieve as long as we are willing to credit others." How true.

In group settings, properly phrase questions and comments. There is very little value in shooting poison-tipped arrows at the other side. There is very little to be gained from unnecessarily hostile, shark-like behavior.

Choose to admit your mistakes and move ahead rather than wasting energy blaming others. This is how you win people over.

Recognize the possibility in the midst of difficulty rather than difficulty in the midst of possibility. There is a lot greater value in "how we can" thinking than "why we can't."

Choose to say "I must . . ." rather than "Someone should . . ." This is how you take ownership and control over your situation. Remember, we are all writing and playing the main character in our own life story. We can't edit the chapters that have already been written, but we can certainly decide how the story unfolds from this point on.

Regardless of your chosen professional field, choose to mutually benefit rather than getting the best of another person. This is how you live an honorable and reputable life. People will line up to be associated with you.

Consider the future potential rather than the past shortcomings and failures. Edison, without any formal education, failed thousands of times on his way to becoming the greatest inventor of all time. He later stated, "I have not failed. I've just found ten thousand ways that won't work." He was also quoted as saying, "Many of life's failures are men who did not realize how close they were to success when they gave up." I wonder how different our lives would be today if Edison had chosen to give up after so many unsuccessful experiments.

When a man's ways are pleasing to the Lord, he makes even his enemies live at peace with him.
—Proverbs 16:7

"Hello," "Thank you," "Good job," "I appreciate you," and "I am sorry" are simple yet powerful phrases. Choose to say them often rather than letting your pride get in the way. The human versions of sharks have great difficulty in saying these welcoming phrases.

Choose to admit that you don't know something rather than blabbering an immediate, made-up, insincere response. You don't have to know all the answers. In the case of Trent Lott, the former majority leader of the U.S. Senate, his ignorant comment praising segregationist Strom Thurmond caused a brief nation-wide uproar and cost him his job in 2002.

I don't know the key to success, but the key to failure is trying to please everybody.
—*Bill Cosby, American comedian and actor*

Respect and admiration must be earned. They do not come automatically with your title. Choose to work hard and be an example for others to follow.

Let go of little things. Forgive others rather than building up hatred. Nothing good ever came of pent-up hatred, but our human history is full of horrible things that resulted from it.

Choose to transform "only if . . ." into "even if . . ." Remember, you are bigger than all obstacles, issues, challenges, or other shark species allowed in your life. There are reasons for the sharks in your life. They are waiting to be conquered by you.

You can be gentle with people and effective at the same time. Show your human side in dealing with others rather than acting like a heartless machine. Whoever said there is nothing personal about business was gravely mistaken. Be vulnerable, be emotional, have a sense of humor, admit past mistakes, and show your soft side. This is how you win respect and admiration.

People will gladly follow you. Choose to be different. Choose to be your good self. Be honorable. You don't have to be a shark to swim with and outswim them.

CHAPTER 19

TAKE CONTROL OF YOUR THOUGHTS, WORDS, AND HABITS

Change your thoughts, and you change your world.
—Norman Vincent Peale, Protestant preacher and author of
The Power of Positive Thinking

I would be remiss if I did not discuss the importance of your thoughts, choice of words, actions, habits, and attitudes as the essential ingredients necessary for properly shaping your life. On multiple occasions, I have read the following:

> *Watch your thoughts, for they become words.*
> *Watch your words, for they become actions.*
> *Watch your actions, for they become habits.*
> *Watch your habits, for they become character.*
> *Watch your character, for it becomes your destiny.*
> *—Anonymous*

This saying is so true. I am sure many of you have heard it before as well. Whoever came up with it is a concise, eloquent, and superb communicator. Yes, we certainly need to carefully choose our thoughts, words, actions, habits, and ultimately our attitudes in order to outswim our sharks and reach success. Nearly two centuries ago, in the early 1800s, Charles Reade, an English novelist and dramatist best known for *The Cloister and the Hearth*, made a very similar statement: "Sow an act and you reap a habit; sow a habit and you reap a character; sow a character and you reap a destiny." Timeless advice.

There are many great books already available reiterating the importance of these key personal traits. There are just as many great books on how to positively change and develop them. To avoid being redundant, let me make two crucial points in my own style, atypical from most other books.

Your Attitude Will Dictate How You View the World

Man of La Mancha, a musical made in 1972, is based on the novel *Don Quixote* by Miguel de Cervantes. This happens to be yet another one of my favorite stories growing up. I must have driven some adults in my neighborhood crazy, trying to mimic the battles in my own unique way.

In this most entertaining story, Don Quixote sees the world as a great adventure. He dreams the impossible, valiantly fights the invisible and the unbeatable enemy, and looks at life as a personal challenge to bring goodness in the midst of evil and make the world a better place.

Don Quixote falls in love with an ordinary kitchen maid. In his mind, he sees her as a lady of most stunning beauty and chastity. He wants to dedicate his hard-fought victories to this amazing and special lady. Unfortunately, she has quite the opposite thoughts and attitudes toward the world. She is full of anger and bitterness. Here's an almost comical conversation between the two from the English-translated version by John Rutherford:

"Why do you do these things?" she asks.

"What things?" Don Quixote inquires.

"It's ridiculous, the things you do!" she screams, her voice full of disbelief and irritation.

"I come from a world of iron to make a world of gold," Don Quixote answers with pride and conviction in his voice.

"The world is a dung heap," she says, "and we are maggots that crawl on it."

Ouch. Talk about poor self-esteem.

What's your reality? How do you choose to view the world? In this classic story, the main character lives a life of purpose, beauty, and adventure. The other views the exact same world with resentment and sees it as filled with utter misery. Yes,

I know. Don Quixote, I admit, was a bit "out there" to say the least. Nevertheless, the story serves as a comical example and as a reminder of how people can view the same world so differently depending on their thoughts and attitudes.

Do you view and treat your life as the most precious gift from our Maker? Or do you resent ever receiving this gift? Do you realize you are a valuable individual with unique talents? Or do you consider yourself one of the countless "maggots" crawling in the deep pile of "dung" called life? You can live your life in any way you choose. Choose to be optimistic. No one has ever achieved anything worthwhile by being pessimistic. Choose to see life's wonders. Choose not to be bitter or hardened by all the bad things that have happened to you in the past. Don't be too disappointed when things don't go your way. There are reasons for the less than ideal circumstances, problems, and all other shark species in your life. They exist to be conquered by you. They are simply temporary stops and minor detours along the way to your success and reaching your full potential. But you won't be able to get through them without a positive outlook in life and unless you believe you can outswim them.

A man is but the product of his thoughts. What he thinks, he becomes.
—Mahatma Gandhi, Indian philosopher, internationally esteemed for his doctrine of nonviolent protest

AS A MAN THINKETH BY JAMES ALLEN

In the early 1900s, a relatively unknown writer and philosopher in rural England wrote a short book, *As a Man Thinketh* (which is actually more like a long article or an essay than a book), which has since become a classic. In naming his masterpiece, he borrowed a passage from Proverbs 23:7: "As a man thinketh in his heart, so is he." The following are excerpts from his writing that I found most relevant to our topic at hand:

- Just as the gardener cultivates his plot, keeping it free from weeds, and growing the flowers and fruits which he requires, so may a man tend the garden of his mind, weeding out all the wrong, useless, and impure thoughts, and cultivating toward perfection the flowers and fruits of right, useful, and pure thoughts. By pursuing this process, a man sooner or later discovers that he is the master-gardener of his soul, the director of his life.

- The outer world of circumstances shapes itself to the inner world of thought, and both pleasant and unpleasant external conditions are factors which make for the ultimate good of the individual. As the reaper of his own harvest, man learns both by suffering and bliss.

- Circumstance does not make the man; it reveals him to himself.

- Not what he wishes and prays for does man get, but what he justly earns. His wishes and prayers are only gratified and answered when they harmonize with his thoughts and actions.

- Good thoughts and actions can never produce bad results; bad thoughts and actions can never produce good results.

- A man only begins to be a man when he ceases to whine and revile, and commences to search for the hidden justice which regulates his life.

- To think well of all, to be cheerful with all, to patiently learn to find the good in all—such unselfish thoughts are the very portals of heaven.

Changing Habits

Have you ever watched the Space Shuttle being launched? It is simply an awesome sight. It is amazing what humans can achieve. Viewing it on TV just isn't the same—the powerful sound, the ground-shaking vibrations, the magnitude of it all; it's hard to fully appreciate the monumental event over the TV screen. Having been an engineer myself once, I would rank this as one of the greatest engineering feats we have ever achieved.

Let me first share some facts regarding space shuttles and then try to link them to our topic at hand. Wish me luck.

The Space Shuttle stands 184 feet high, comparable to the height of a sixteen-story building. At launch, it consists of a rust-colored external tank, two white, slender solid rocket boosters, and the orbiter, which, for the most part, resembles an airplane.

The shuttle starts its mission with a mass of more than 4.4 million pounds. Most of this is the fuel required for proper takeoff. To put things in perspective, this mass is equivalent to approximately 1,400 midsize automobiles or thirty Boeing 737 planes. Yes, the Space Shuttle is enormous.

Once out of the earth's orbit, the cruising speed for this massive and marvelous human creation reaches 17,000 miles per hour. This is almost five miles per second. At this speed, one could travel from Seoul to Los Angeles in a mere twenty minutes, and from New York to London in about twelve minutes. Yes, an incredible speed. I once had a somewhat absentminded physics teacher back in high school who claimed that the Space Shuttle astronauts age significantly less than we earthlings while traveling in outer space at these great speeds. I suppose Einstein really knew his stuff. I wonder if we can use this argument for increasing or altogether eliminating highway speed limits. Hmm.

Back to the point. To work itself up to this unbelievable speed, the Space Shuttle starts off at a pace equally slow and tortoise-like. It barely moves at first. You hold your breath as it desperately fights gravity and literally inches its way up. It's so slow that if you had never seen a launch before, you would doubt whether this gigantic structure was capable of overcoming the mighty forces of gravity and making it to its destined full ascent. In the first few moments, as it claws its way up, it burns massive amounts of fuel. The two solid rocket boosters need to generate a thrust of

12.5 meganewtons each (2.8 million pounds of force). To help you put this in perspective, the total 25 million meganewtons worth of force is a whopping 950 times the thrust generated by a Boeing 737 airplane. It takes a lot to get this thing going, but with certain and ever-increasing ease, the shuttle picks up and roars into the clear sky, headed into space and reaching its intended speed of 17,000 miles per hour.

Men acquire a particular quality by constantly acting a particular way . . . you become just by performing just actions, temperate by performing temperate actions, brave by performing brave actions.
—Aristotle, ancient Greek philosopher, student of Plato, and teacher of Alexander the Great

Within the first one hundred seconds of its launch, the Space Shuttle exhausts 80 percent of the fuel. Yes, 80 percent of the fuel in the first one hundred seconds. This is what must be done just to get it moving upward. Take comfort, however; once it gains enough momentum after the first two minutes or so, keeping the shuttle moving is relatively easy and takes very little fuel. It's smooth sailing the rest of the way if you can endure the anticipated arduous beginning. This is true for us as well.

What bad habits do you have? What good habits do you lack? I define bad habits to be those that hinder you from reaching your goals. In contrast, as you can imagine, good habits are those that will help you attain your worthwhile goals. What habits do you need to abort or launch to realize your maximum potential altitude? Get off the ground. Once we shed our bad habits and acquire the right ones, we will be able to enjoy the spectacular view from way up high.

I know it's extremely difficult to change habits formed over many years. Whether we like it or not, achieving our goals often requires dramatic changes in our habits. It took a concerned doctor sitting me down to warn me of the dangers of high cholesterol levels before I changed my diet and started a regular cardiovascular workout regime. It took the threat of divorce before a close colleague changed his ways for the better. It cost another acquaintance bankruptcy before adopting sound spending habits. The vast majority of us have at least one bad habit grounding us. We have allowed, or perhaps even nurtured, our bad habit to become one of the biggest sharks in our lives. One good habit may be what lies between us and our success.

Fix your habits to be consistent with your life goals. Expect it to be hard during the initial launch phase. Be reasonable about the duration. No, you can't stop smoking for a hundred seconds and expect it to be smooth sailing the rest of the way. Give it a few months. Give it all you have during this takeoff phase. Practice better eating habits. Force yourself to get up thirty minutes earlier. Work on your tone of voice. Be friendlier. Smile more; frown less. Follow up on the commitment to spend more quality time with your loved ones. Criticize less and praise more often. Learn to speak less and listen more.

Expect it to be difficult for the first few months. If you can endure and persist during the initial launch phase, I assure you, it will be much, much easier the rest of the way. In fact, you will most likely have developed a new habit you urgently need to reach your goals.

As you create your own life story, what attitudes do you want your main character (that would be you) to have? Are you heroic enough? Or are you too weak? Are you giving in too early or too easily to the problems of this world? Remind yourself that you were never intended to be shark bait. Do you have a definite sense of destiny and purpose in your own life story? Or is your story turning out to be a nebulous one without any substantial or meaningful plot? You can't go back and rewrite the previous chapters, but fortunately, you can control how the story flows from this point on. You have the right and the ability to mold your desired ending. Create your own masterpiece.

Start with thinking the right thoughts and doing the right things until they become your habits. To reach our full potential, we must align our thoughts, words, actions, and habits properly.

CHAPTER 20
BE A ROLE MODEL

If you can tell me who your heroes are,

I can tell you how you are going to turn out in life.

—*Warren Buffet, investor, businessman, and philanthropist*

Who's your role model? Who's your hero? I don't mean Superman, Spiderman, or any other made-up superheroes. I'm asking for your real-life hero, someone you look up to, someone you respect, someone you aspire to be.

It's a good idea to have one or two. It is even better if the person is easily accessible to you. Admiring a deceased historical figure isn't as desirable since this person may have lived in a completely different time and environment. The person is not available to give you practical advice, and you will be limited to what you read in books.

A hero can be just about anyone: your parent, a relative, a former teacher, someone at work, or any other person you had the fortunate chance to meet. Arbitrary classifications we often like to use, such as race and age, aren't important. Your role model needs to be someone with your desired qualities and whose life you would like to emulate. Consider yourself fortunate if you already have a role model in your life.

Are You a Hero?

Now let's consider the flip side. Who would name you as their role model? Do your peers respect you? What would your subordinates say about you to their closest friends? What does your boss think of you? What would your former teachers say about you? If you are married, do you have the respect of your spouse? Do your kids look up to you? Do you have the adoration of your loved ones? How have you positively impacted their lives? Are you proud of yourself? Are your responses to these questions consistent with how you want to be remembered?

What you do speaks so loudly that I cannot hear what you say.
—Ralph Waldo Emerson, American essayist, philosopher, and poet

You should serve as a role model to at least one person you love. This is an indication that you are living a worthwhile life and, equivalently, that you are making a positive difference in someone else's life. If no one in this world considers you a role model, perhaps it would prove prudent to reevaluate your life. Start by revisiting your life goals.

Improve Yourself Before Advising Others

I once read the story of a troubled mother who took her daughter to see Gandhi. Gandhi was already well known and world renowned for his great spiritual discipline. It seemed the young girl had become addicted to eating sweets, and her mother wanted Gandhi to speak to her about this harmful habit and convince her to stop it. Upon hearing this simple request, Gandhi paused in deep silence and then told the mother to bring her daughter back in three weeks, when he would speak with her. Just as she was instructed, the mother returned with her daughter, and Gandhi, as he had promised, spoke to the girl about the detrimental effects of eating too many sweets. He gently and effectively counseled her to give them up.

The mother gratefully thanked Gandhi but remained perplexed. "Why," she asked, "did you not speak to my daughter when we first came to you?" "My good woman," Gandhi replied, "three weeks ago I myself was still addicted to sweets!"

Every day we face circumstances that provide us with the golden opportunity to set an example for others to follow. You can't be a role model if you choose to act and react with the majority in difficult situations. Choose to be the spark of optimism in the spreading fire of cynicism and gloom. Choose to be the desperately needed beacon of light in the pitch darkness of despair.

Don't worry that children never listen to you. Worry that they are always watching you.
—*Robert Fulghum, author of*
All I Really Need to Know
I Learned in Kindergarten

Show compassion and kindness when others are most concerned about meeting selfish needs. Demonstrate hard work when others are busy looking for an easy way out. Epitomize integrity when the majority is content going with the flow.

You don't have to be a shark to swim with and outswim them. You certainly don't have to act like them. Stand firm in your principles. Act consistently with your high moral standards. Let others learn from you. Be a role model.

CHAPTER 21
START NOW!

The great French Marshall Lyautey once asked his gardener to plant a tree.

The gardener objected that the tree was slow growing and would not

reach maturity for 100 years. The Marshall replied, "In that case,

there is no time to lose; plant it this afternoon!"

—*John F. Kennedy, thirty-fifth president of the United States*

We aren't getting any younger. It's such an old cliché, but unfortunately, it's true. At this precise moment, you are the youngest you will ever be for the rest of your life. I know, it's a scary thought. I can hardly believe I am already in my forties. I vividly remember thinking thirty was old. And time only travels in one direction, except in movies and science fiction. The ever-increasing gray hair on my head serves as a constant and cruel reminder of this fact every morning.

Life is too short to have regrets. Dive in. Seize the opportunity that's been given to you. Change the course you are currently on to follow your dreams. Keeping in mind what's most important to you, set your goals and pursue them with all your might. Take the new career path you have always wanted—even if it means taking a reduction in pay. Money should represent merely one of many variables, a small one at that, in making the right decisions. You can make up financial losses later in life, but time lost can never be regained. Determine what's most important to you. Live today consistently with how you want to be remembered when you are no longer around.

Would you like to be remembered as someone who always played it safe? Someone who never took chances in life? There is nothing wrong with playing it safe. But most people I know have far more regrets about what they didn't do than what they did in the past. I don't want to be on my deathbed wondering what my life could have been. Take charge and live a life you were meant to and want to live.

There is so much to do and so many lives to touch along the way. There is no time for laziness and procrastination. Yes, I am sure there are many obstacles and challenges in your life. These sharks won't go away by themselves. Choose to conquer them and take action toward your life dreams. Start today. You can't change the past, but you can influence and shape your future in any way you choose.

Is It Too Late?

Perhaps you are thinking it's too late for you. Consider the following people who made historical contributions late in life.

Benjamin Franklin, who played a crucial role in drafting the Declaration of Independence, was seventy when he signed it. He signed the Constitution of the United States of America at age eighty-one. Ronald Reagan became the governor of California in his late fifties and later became the fortieth U.S. president when he was seventy. Winston Churchill was sixty-five when he became Prime Minister of the United

Though no one can go back and make a brand new start, anyone can start from now and make a brand new end.
—Carl Bard, Scottish theologian and writer

Kingdom and remained active and productive until his death at age ninety.

Leonardo da Vinci penned many of his famous sketches in his sixties. Michelangelo sculpted into his eighties. John Ogilby, the translator of Homer and Virgil, started learning Latin and Greek in his midfifties. Leo Tolstoy wrote novels into his seventies. Chaucer wrote his *Canterbury Tales* in his late fifties. Johann Wolfgang von Goethe, often considered Germany's greatest literary figure, completed *Faust*, arguably his greatest work, in his eighties.

There are examples in sports as well, where you would expect age to equate to reduced performance. Randy Johnson, often referred to as the "Big Unit" due to his enormous stature of 6 feet 10 inches, comes to my mind. As a side note, a friend's wife was actually Randy Johnson's personal chef for a while. In fact, my buddy Paul and his wife first met at a baseball game when she had access to the box seats given to her by Randy Johnson. I suppose you never know whom you will meet at any given moment in life.

Let me get back to the Randy Johnson story. He is undoubtedly one of the best Major League Baseball pitchers of all time. He has almost 5,000 strikeouts (second in Major League history) and has won the Cy Young Award five times (second only to the seven won by Roger Clemens). His greatest performance was on May 18, 2004, when he pitched a perfect game against the Atlanta Braves. In the Major League's 132-year history, there had only been sixteen other perfect games—if you do the math, this equates to one perfect game every eight years, or about every 11,000 games. It's a career-making accomplishment most pitchers dream of. What's even more impressive is that he was only a few months away from turning forty-one, way past normal retirement age in professional sports. Despite being an outstanding player for many years, Randy Johnson's greatest baseball moment came toward the very end of his famed career.

I could go on and on with examples, but I'm pretty sure you get my point. Whatever your goals are, it's never too late to pursue them. Most people give up as the years pass. They think it's too late. Perhaps this very negative thought is the biggest shark in your life that you first and foremost need to defeat. You can believe otherwise. Your personal best and your greatest moment in life have yet to come. In the words of Robert Browning, English poet and playwright, "Grow old along with me! The best is yet to be . . . Trust God: see all, nor be afraid!"

It's not too late to be a better person going forward. You can be a better, more loving spouse. You can be a better parent to your kids. You can be a better friend whom people can depend on. You can be a better coworker whom people enjoy being with. You can be a better, more respectable boss. You can be a better, more active listener. You can be in better shape. If you are willing, you can change your attitude and outlook on life. It's not too late. The choice has always been and will remain yours and yours alone. Your greatest moment and your greatest achievement in life lie in your future, not in the past—but only if you let them. Get started now.

EPILOGUE

The vast majority of us are so busy living that we hardly ever get a chance to reflect on what we are living for. The world is full of broken dreams and lost souls. Many of us are driving aimlessly and meandering through our lives without a clear purpose or ultimate destination. Some of us may have started with a destination in mind but have since allowed distractions, adversities, unexpected events, naysayers, and many other shark species to derail us from our path. You don't have to be one of them. You have the option to create the story of your own life in any way you choose.

There are reasons for the sharks in our lives. They are allowed in our lives to be conquered by us and to enrich our own lives and those of others. There is a better and stronger you waiting on the other side.

Write your own inspirational and touching life story with yourself as the hero. Use your life as the blank page. Create a masterpiece. Turn your life into a great comeback story that others will refer to and use to improve their own lives. It's never too early, and it's never too late. You can't change your past, but you have direct control and input on how your own story flows from this point forward. With focus, determination, and hard work, you can and will overcome whatever tragedies and setbacks you have encountered. You can outswim the sharks in your life if you choose to make the necessary sacrifices. You are bigger and stronger than any of the shark species allowed in your life.

Dream big dreams. We are often more capable than we give ourselves credit for. Also, dream the right dreams. We get to live our lives only once. Make sure you live an honorable one, worthy of our Maker's intentions. Envision your bright future and work diligently and relentlessly toward your dreams despite and in the midst of your sharks. With hard work, learn to replace your fear of potential failure with expectations of deserved success.

Whatever your worthwhile goals are, start on them today. At this precise moment, you are the youngest you will ever be for the rest of your life. Make sure today does not become the past that you will come to regret later in your life.

Thank you for reading this book. I hope you enjoyed it as much as I enjoyed writing it. I will consider my goals to have been met if you found this book helpful with any of the following three things:

1. Defining your own set of worthwhile life goals by examining what's truly important to you and how you ultimately want to be remembered. This is of utmost importance. We first need a dream before we can chase and achieve it. As I speak with and counsel others, I am stunned by how many people live without a clear purpose or goal in their lives. Just as we should have a clear destination in mind before we start driving, we should have clear life goals for the rest of our lives.

2. Swimming with and outswimming your sharks without succumbing or resorting to their ways. There will always be sharks in your life. There are so many people who allow their sharks to shape their attitude, personality, outlook, and approach to life. They allow their sharks to dictate their behavior and actions. To succeed, you cannot let these sharks distract you. You must not succumb, but rather must overcome them to reach your goals.

3. Evaluating your life regularly to make sure you are on track and making progress toward the desired ending in your own life story. You are the main character in the story of your life. You are also the author. You have the choice to make it into any story you wish. Create a masterpiece life story for yourself.

ABOUT THE AUTHOR

Joong ("Joon") H. Hyun was born in Seoul, immigrated to the United States at a young age, and has since worked and lived in numerous countries in the Americas, Europe, and Asia.

For the past two decades, Joong has worked with many global Fortune 500 companies in various capacities. His experiences include working as a managing director for an international consultancy, as vice president of Global Strategy, and as vice president of the Asia region for a multibillion-dollar, U.S.-based company. He received his undergraduate degree from Virginia Tech, master's degree from Northwestern, and MBA from Carnegie Mellon.

Your comments and feedback on this book will be very much appreciated. Suggestions for future books are also encouraged. Joong can be reached at either joong.h.hyun@quantigate.com or joong.h.hyun@gmail.com.